SNOW IN THE TROPICS

I was born in Kent on a fruit farm in 1929, and during the war my parents sent my brother and me to boarding schools to get us away from the bombing, first to Somerset and then to Northamptonshire.

I spent a year in Canada after leaving school before joining my father on the farm. Having missed National Service on account of my occupation, I joined the Territorial Army which was life so far removed from farming that the two week annual camp was almost as good as a holiday.

I played rugby on Saturdays during the winter until I broke my leg in a skiing accident, and then took up golf, which I still play with great enthusiasm and little skill.

My father died in 1956, and I ran the farm until I sold it in 1989. I did voluntary work for the Citizens Advice Bureau during my retirement until we moved to Bangkok.

For Anne

SNOW IN THE TROPICS

with love

Gun

May 2012

Guy Snow

SNOW IN THE TROPICS

Seven memorable years in and around Bangkok

Olympia Publishers

www.olympiapublishers.com
OLYMPIA PAPERBACK EDITION

A CIP catalogue record for this title is
available from the British Library.

ISBN: 978-1-84897-013-7

Olympia Publishers part of Ashwell Publishing Ltd.

First Published in 2009

Olympia Publishers
60 Cannon Street
London
EC4N 6NP

Printed in Great Britain

I dedicate this book to my wife Bridget, whose appointment to teach in Bangkok gave me this amazing opportunity to taste the delights of the Land of Smiles. And of course the way in which she proof-read and corrected the schoolboy errors in my text.

CONTENTS

CHAPTER 1

Leaving the UK

"How would you like to live in Bangkok?" These were the words with which Bridget greeted me when she returned from school one day in July 1997. Slightly bemused, I said "OK,." and waited to hear what it was all about.

She was teaching seven and eight-year-olds in a school near Tonbridge in Kent where one Stuart Morris was the head. It transpired that he had been 'headhunted' to start up an International School in Bangkok under the sponsorship of Harrow School, and it was to open in 1998. Tongue (slightly) in cheek, Bridget offered her services as a year two teacher, and Stuart welcomed her as his first recruit.

Having sold the farm that had been in my family for over 100 years when I retired seven years earlier, we were rattling around in the six-bedroom farmhouse (which was not wanted by the buyer of the land) and we had vaguely had the idea that we should perhaps move to a smaller property with our twelve-year-old son, Edward. So this seemed to be an opportunity thrust upon us.

Selling the house, storing the furniture and moving into temporary rented accommodation is an episode of my life that I would rather draw a veil over, because it was so stressful. I have been really lucky not to have had to move far in my time, as I have always lived on or near the farm, and this was an eye-opener.

We put the sale of the property into the hands of an agent in Maidstone, and they sent out a photographer who spent all day waiting for the right light conditions for portraying the outside of the house. In the meantime he took photographs of the inside, and I had to light fires in the large inglenook fireplaces in both the sitting room and the dining room, so that the rooms looked homely and cosy. This operation used up about a month's worth of firewood, and as I had no more apple wood from the farm I would have had to buy some more had it not been April, when we had finished with fires. Then we needed to lay the dining room table as though we were about to have a dinner party for twelve guests. I must say that the pictures looked lovely when we saw them, and we would have felt tempted to make an offer should we want to buy this sort of property ourselves.

During the next couple of months I showed round several prospective buyers and I soon learnt to distinguish between those who were serious and those who were just having an afternoon out. One couple seemed very enthusiastic, both of whom had jobs in mid Kent, but after a second visit when they brought their small children to see it, the husband phoned later to say that they could not proceed because his wife found the stairs were 'non-standard'. We had two staircases, one of which was spiral, encased in a stair tower, and had been added on to the fifteenth century house in the sixteenth century. The other was admittedly steep and narrow, but the building regulations of four or five hundred years ago were probably not so strict as they are today. This was a pity, because not only did I think that the house would suit the family, but I thought that the family would suit the house.

Another viewer wanted to do away with the small cellar by filling it with rubble or even concrete. This horrified me, as I had been particularly fond of this part of the house, which kept an even temperature all year round. But who was I to make a judgement on other people's alterations? Eventually the house was sold to a buyer who kept on procrastinating until I threatened to withdraw, and so we no longer owned any property in Leeds – or anywhere else for that matter!

The next thing was to engage a removal and storage firm, who delivered a large number of boxes which we started to fill. Seeing all our possessions packed into boxes was very distressing, as I was totally unable to sift those which we needed to keep from those which were easily replaced. I can't believe that I packed old tobacco tins full of rusty screws and nails which I had been keeping for the day when they would 'come in useful'! But I did, and the consequence of this was that we found ourselves with nine containers of about eight or nine cubic metres each for storage. Three full lorry loads. But this turned out to be not nearly as traumatic as the day, some two years later, when we sorted these down into three containers.

The rented accommodation that we had arranged turned out to be unavailable, as the owners were having some improvements made to the property which hadn't been finished. So at very short notice we had to find somewhere else, and this was a holiday let and quite expensive for four weeks. It was in fact very comfortable, and ideally placed in the middle of Horsmonden opposite the pub, so we enjoyed this phase rather more than the original property, which we moved into in Northiam for a further four weeks, but which cost half as much.

So having arranged with the HSBC for our assets to provide for us from now on, we set off for Bangkok from Heathrow by EVA Air at 9.30 in the evening of Thursday, 4th August 1998, arriving at 3.30 the following afternoon.

CHAPTER 2

Arrival in Bangkok

Stuart met us at the airport, and having sorted out a lost suitcase, we found his car for the drive to the apartments where we were to live for the next week. The first thing that struck us when we left the air-conditioned airport was the heat. August is one of the hottest and most humid times of the year, and the temperature of 35°C and more, with high humidity, can be quite debilitating to some, but it was something that we both enjoyed. Although it has to be said that the 'cool' season of December and January, when the mercury is around 28°C, is on the whole more pleasant.

The school (for a variety of reasons) was in the process of moving to another site, and within a week we were installed in what turned out to be our home for the next seven years – the fifteenth floor of Bangkok Garden Apartments. I don't think that I had been as high as this before except in an aeroplane, but we quickly got used to it. However, the lift never broke down, and I wonder what state we would have been in had we had to climb the stairs with our shopping in the heat of the day!

As it was the school holidays, we were able to explore Bangkok; and what a city it is! The Chao Phraya river, which is wide, dirty and very lively, is full of barges towed by little tugs going upstream and downstream, empty or full of rice, sand, rubble, fuel and anything else that is bulky. Full, the decks are awash, and going upstream against the flow they seem to make little progress. Empty, they stand 20 or 30 feet out of the water. Timber is usually floated downstream in rafts, with men scampering about on the logs to keep them together. Fascinating to watch, I never saw anyone fall into the water, and could only wonder at their fate if they did.

All day long the river buses are plying their trade, and are full to overflowing between six and eight in the morning with city workers starting their day, and again between six and eight in the evening going home, and at all other times busy with tourists. If you live and work near the river, this is an ideal way of travelling, as the roads in the city are pretty busy, to put it mildly. These buses are operated by a driver who sits in the front, and a crewman who stands at the back and gives signals with a whistle for the driver to draw alongside each jetty. On many occasions, when there are few passengers, the boat hardly stops at all before it accelerates away to the next stop. Eight baht (about 11 pence) takes you anywhere, and is collected by a girl with a roll of tickets and a machine with which to validate them, which goes 'ping'. Shut your eyes, and you could be on a 1950s London bus (no, not really!).

Long narrow boats are operated privately and are called 'long-tails' on account of the propeller being at the end of a long shaft. Driven by a noisy V8 engine, the boat is steered by the boatman moving the whole of the engine and shaft from side to side. They skim along at quite a pace carrying anything from one to twelve passengers up and down the river, and along the canals for sightseeing; this is the most relaxing way of seeing some interesting parts of Bangkok for not a great deal of money. They are difficult to get in and out of for a geriatric like me, but well worth the effort and worry that you might fall into the water after a missed step. Falling into the Chao Phraya river is definitely not recommended as the water is filthy, and in fact when speeding along it is even advisable to protect your lips from the spray from the bow wave!

Once ashore, you realize how big the city really is. What looks like a short walk on the map is really quite a long way, and thus we made our way up the entire length of Silom Road where the HSBC building was located, as we wanted to open an account. Your nostrils are assaulted at every turn with alternately delicious and disgusting smells. Bangkok is only a foot or two above sea level, and was originally networked by canals (thus its name of the Venice of the East); many of these have been paved over to make roads, but by leaving them full of stagnant water, these are a constant source of malodour to say the least. On the other hand, everywhere there are food vendors tending their portable kitchens, which give off a stream of mouthwatering smells. It is said that Thais only have one meal a day – they start at 8 a.m. and finish at 8 p.m! In fact, they are always 'grazing', and eat little and often; I saw few fat Thais and their diet of rice, vegetables, meat or fish in a stir-fried dish is pretty healthy. There is, however, a generation of teenagers and those in their early twenties who patronize fast food outlets such as the omnipresent McDonalds, and there are quite a few chubby members in this age group.

Eventually arriving at the HSBC offices, I had my male pride dented for the first time when I found out that as Bridget had a work permit and I had not, she had to be the account holder, and I was an additional signatory. Banking is not made easy for the ordinary person here, and that is probably why so many transactions are made in cash – even for large sums like 100,000 baht which I paid to the travel agent for three return flights each summer.

Driving in Bangkok, especially on the expressways, is like being in a video game. Vehicles overtake from all sides and change lanes at the drop of a hat – often with no warning whatsoever. If there is more than one car's length available in front of you, someone will fill it, and once you realize this, you either drive really close to the car in front, or leave a sensible gap and don't complain. Drivers do not seem to be too concerned with what is going on behind them, but only where they can exploit the next opportunity in front. Occasionally a small pick-up truck will speed through the traffic ignoring all the rules by which Thais seem to drive; these are on their way to collect a body before someone else does, but we only ever saw one on the road, and that was roughly covered with newspaper. Having said all this, I have to say that on the whole they have a very healthy respect for the rain and wet roads.

There is an excellent network of elevated expressways over and around Bangkok, and apart from being able to avoid the choked up roads at street level, the best thing is that motorbikes are not allowed on them. These bikes are an absolute menace in the city to road users and pedestrians alike, and are everywhere. Mind you, it is a very efficient way to travel amongst largely stationary traffic, and journey times can be a fraction of that taken by three and four wheeled vehicles, although journey time to your maker can also be hastened as motorbike accidents are by far and away the highest cause of death on the roads in Thailand.

I took a couple of rides, but only because time was a factor. With no helmet on, I feared my spectacles would blow off if I moved my head, so I took them off when we stopped at some traffic lights, and put them in my pocket. When we started again, I found that I had a fly or a piece of grit in my eye, and as my hands were fully occupied in gripping the handle behind my pillion seat, I shut my eyes until the end of the journey. This, I decided, was probably the best way to travel on a motorbike!

Motorbikes seem to have few traffic laws which apply to them. True, there is a helmet law, but the few bikers who wore them seemed to think that a tin hat of sorts was adequate (in fact this law was more widely observed and policed by the time we left Bangkok). All the same, it was very disquieting to see a whole family of four or five perched on a single two-stroke bike with only the driver wearing any sort of headgear. It is as though nobody was aware that children's skulls were only about as tough as eggshells. Again it is true that the rule of the road requires you to drive on the left, and fortunately this is observed by cars, but you frequently meet a motorcyclist coming towards you in the gutter, who may or may not have his lights on after dark. Pavements are for pedestrians mainly, and on the whole cars don't drive on them, but motorbikes do, and it is most unnerving to see one coming towards you. It is even more unnerving suddenly to hear them coming up behind you!

Another rule of the road which one quickly learns to obey is that lorries and buses have the right of way over cars. As far as I know, this is not written down anywhere, but as they are bigger than you, this seems a sensible rule to follow! Anyway, in the event of an accident, a 'farang' (foreigner) is always in the wrong, and the hassle that it causes is not worth the trouble of insisting that it was 'your right of way'.

'Tuk-tuks' are so named on account of the noise made by their two-stroke gas fuelled engines, and they are nearly as much of a menace as motorbikes. With the driver sitting astride the engine and steering a single front wheel with handlebars, the passengers sit on a bench seat over the two back wheels. There is really only enough room for two people but we often travelled with three, but it is common to see five, six and more youngsters sharing the fare. This has to be negotiated with the driver before you set off, as they do not have meters, and it is important to know roughly what the cost of a taxi fare would be for the same journey. They are really rather over-rated but, as one of the sights of Bangkok, must be experienced. There is only a roof with no side curtains, and if it rains, you get wet. For a normal sized farang your head touches the roof, and it is impossible to see anything above the first floor of buildings unless you put your head outside – which is highly inadvisable! Added to this, when stationary in a traffic jam, you are quite likely to have a lorry or bus next to you pumping filthy exhaust fumes into your face through a six-inch exhaust pipe. It can be quite fun late at night when a party of you take two tuk-tuks home, and the drivers take it into their heads to have a race, though this can be rather scary, as they appear to be pretty unstable at the best of times.

The *Bangkok Post* – one of the two most widely read English language newspapers in Bangkok, the other being *The Nation* – published a list of road rules poking fun at the police, which is worth repeating:

1. Ensure your vehicle comes to full halt before paying bribe.

2. Drivers of luxury European cars are not required to stop at police checkpoints.

3. If involved in a minor traffic accident, try to ensure that at least two lanes of traffic are blocked, and do not move vehicles until the police arrive 3 hours later.

4. Sounding horn to wake up officer manning police traffic booth to get him to switch the lights to green is prohibited.

5. Give way to bus drivers fleeing the scene of an accident.

6. Motor cyclists must wear crash helmets sometimes.

7. Be considerate and allow short people and old ladies to the front of the crowd at horrific accident scenes.

8. Exercise care while driving under the influence of alcohol, especially if talking on a mobile phone.

9. It is mandatory for motorcyclists to switch on headlights during daylight hours. Switching them on at night time is optional.

10. A series of evenly spaced black and white rectangular markings found on the road are known as pedestrian crossings. Ignore them.

Foreigners, especially white-skinned ones, are very vulnerable to being targeted by the police for real or imaginary traffic infringements – particularly towards the end of the month when their pay cheques are due.

For my first offence, I had unwittingly driven up a right-turn-only lane when intending to go straight on. Unfortunately there was a police box at that very junction, and a policeman came out of it and invited me inside. This I did, and he started slowly writing out a ticket while explaining my offence in halting English; not quite knowing the form, I took out my wallet to show him my licence. It was when he started fingering the money inside that I realised that he was not really interested in my licence at all, so I gave him a 500 baht note (about seven pounds 50p) which he deftly slipped under his report pad, and immediately tore up the form he had started writing. With that, he escorted me back to the car, held up the traffic while I backed into the flow and off I went to a smart salute. I think 500 baht was probably over the top, and on subsequent occasions got away with 200!

CHAPTER 3

Around Bangkok

There is a weekend market in Chatuchak which has to be visited at least once when in Bangkok, and we went there several times not only to take our guests, but also to pick up some pretty good bargains. The area is jam-packed with stalls cheek by jowl with one another selling an unimaginable range of goods: clothes, of course, shoes, leather goods, china, glass, plants ranging from cut flowers to small trees, animals, birds, snakes, toys, watches and other jewellery, bolts of cloth from many different ethnic sources, antiques and much more.

Stalls selling the same things were clustered together, but as they all looked the same, it was very easy to become disorientated. Nowhere were prices marked up, and the price of everything depended on how much the buyer was prepared to spend, and bargaining was the order of the day. The dealer would ask for a sum of money and Bridget would reply in Thai, and as soon as they heard a foreigner speaking their own language, they would halve the asking price, so she did most of the buying for our friends!

Food stalls abound in order to satisfy the Thai passion for grazing, selling rice dishes with mainly chicken, eggs and pork cooked in a wok on a gas or charcoal stove. We ate at these places all over Bangkok, and we were never ill as a result, though we did have a very unfortunate experience once in

Burma. (Our gastro-intestinal problems were usually related to alcohol!) There was a delightful bar in the middle of the market somewhere – we only ever found it by stumbling upon it – and there was nearly always someone we knew already there, so it was a very sociable place to be. The staff spoke English, and served up a lovely gin and tonic which was very welcome after a couple of hours tramping about the narrow alleyways in the increasing midday heat.

In Bangkok the traffic is always bad, and parking at Chatuchak is impossible after about nine o'clock in the morning, so we always went by taxi until the elevated sky-train was built and then we had cheap, easy and quick transport available. The market only operated on Saturdays and Sundays but we went up there during the week sometimes to walk round the delightful and underused park nearby. There are other parks around, one very small one being near our home, adjacent to the Rama IX bridge. We often went here, and we used to walk round the path marked out in metres which was mainly used by joggers, and we preferred to walk in the opposite direction to the markings in order to see them coming! Situated right alongside the Chao Phraya river, this was a very peaceful area laid out with trees and grass, and when we had walked enough we sat and watched the traffic moving up and down the river.

Lumpini Park is a little larger and much busier and is in the middle of the business district. Lots of office workers take their lunches there in the middle of the day, and joggers and cyclists are constantly on the move over the paths. And of course there are several areas serving food, as always in Thailand.

Nearby is the Snake Farm, where many poisonous snakes are kept for their venom which is extracted on a regular basis. Demonstrations take place during the day where keepers bring king cobras out and tease them with a hooked stick before grabbing them behind the head and holding them so that their fangs pierce some clingfilm stretched over a small bottle. This is then taken to a farm where it is injected into horses which are kept especially for the purpose, and in due course up to a gallon of blood is withdrawn and this is the antidote used when a human is bitten.

A little way out of Bangkok is a crocodile farm where these beasts are bred for shoes and handbags, but is a great tourist attraction – at least once anyway. Thousands of crocodiles lie around motionless in the water or on the concrete surrounds of the pools until twice a day when they are fed, and for a few moments they become quite frenzied and frightening. Most of the viewing is from elevated walkways, and if you drop your hat or handbag then it stays there, consequently parents hold the hands of their children very tightly!

Two of the attendants give a display twice a day of wrestling with their charges, keeping well out of the way of their flashing tails at one end, and their snapping jaws at the other. Finally one of the attendants puts his head in the jaws of one of them – a pretty scary finale.

The Ancient City at Muang Boran is a more restful place to visit. It is an area more or less in the shape of Thailand, and has replicas of important buildings in appropriate places, including a floating market in which are housed the inevitable cafes amongst the tourist shops. There is an old street with houses to walk through, and a shadow puppet theatre – which was a popular form of entertainment in the old days.

Thais lived very simply, and their houses were often built for family groups with three, four or more bedrooms, a kitchen and a central community room, all made of teak. It was not important for the doors or windows to fit to exclude draughts as these were welcome to keep the place cool, and the roof often had a double ridge to aid ventilation. Most doors had a 12-inch sill on which you mustn't tread, and which was put there to prevent evil spirits entering the house. You must step over it, otherwise these little critters who are always lurking and looking out for the main chance, will see you treading on it and gain entry themselves, thus creating bad luck and mayhem for you. Another custom is to take your shoes off before entering a house or temple as the soles of your shoes are considered to be dirty and insulting to a Thai.

The Floating Market at Damnoen Saduak, about an hour or so south of Bangkok, is one of the more charming ways of spending a day out, and we took all our guests there at one time or another. As most transport in old times was along canals in the large central plain of Thailand, the farmers and traders found it convenient to sell their produce from their boats, and the market at Damnoen Saduak is one of the few remaining, though now as a tourist attraction. The main waterway is crowded with flat-bottomed boats piled high with fruit, vegetables, sunhats, toys and souvenirs of all sorts. Amongst them are boats selling food and drinks (of course!), and the boatman – usually a middle-aged woman – sits cross-legged in the stern, often wearing a conical sunhat, slowly paddling her craft up and down selling her wares mainly to tourists. There is at least one large emporium on each side of the waterway selling clothes, pictures and other souvenirs, which are always buzzing with customers.

The market becomes very busy by mid-morning, and we always left home at around six o'clock just as the sun was getting up, and after a hassle-free journey parked the car about five miles from the village where we arranged with a boatman for a negotiated fee (by about ten o'clock people were queuing up, and the fee was definitely non-negotiable!) to take us to the market. Travelling along the intricate network of canals, or klongs, one can observe isolated houses in small plots of land with chicken, geese and pigs, and the occupier very often asleep in a hammock on his balcony, or washing himself in the canal. Plantations of coconuts, each row separated by a ditch flooded for irrigation, alternated with dense jungle in which lurked heaven knows what. Flowering shrubs were everywhere, and there was always something in bloom, but the overall colour was green-laced with the black of the canal water. It is an entirely restful experience, with the hot sun filtering through the overhead canopy in the cool of the morning.

Returning by the same boat to the car some two hours later was a welcome change from the frenetic activity in the centre of the village. We transferred to a small flat-bottomed boat to be paddled up and down the waterway having to weave between traders and tourists alike, and as soon as we got in we were told not to hold on to the sides of the boat and when we saw how close they got to one another, we saw why! It could be very painful. This area is very productive, and going home a different way we passed many banana plantations and market gardens, as well as fruit orchards, all looking extremely well kept.

Ayuttya, one and a half hours north of Bangkok, was one of our favourite places to visit. Capital of Thailand – or Siam as it was then – it was the seat of the Royal Family from the fourteenth to the eighteenth century; this city had always been at war with Burma, and in about 1750 it was completely overrun and sacked. The king fled south and founded Bangkok, then the site of a small fishing village.

Larger than London in its heyday, temples and palaces built of stone and brick were everywhere, and now only crumbling floors and walls survive, which have been made safe for visitors to walk around (and on) amongst the shady trees and grass. One or two of the temples have been restored - one in particular as war reparations by the Burmese some 200 years late!

Nearby was an old elephant corral where the wild animals were herded for taming and training into beasts of burden, and there were some stables here where the elephants lived who gave rides to visitors. We used to go here to watch these amazing animals bathing in the river with their mahouts, and it was great to see them so obviously enjoying themselves. There were always a number of babies here, and it was lovely to see how the mothers looked after them, and even scolded them if they misbehaved.

There was a very small garden centre here as well, which sold a few plants, but the main item of interest was a solid plate-sized object, which you stood in the soil of your pot plants, called 'Eli-poo'. It was, of course, dried elephant dung which I think was more of a talking point than a fertilizer!

CHAPTER 4

Religion and Festivals

There is a wealth of religious buildings and artifacts in Thailand. The Temples – or Wats – are beautifully decorated both inside and out with plenty of loving care and lots of gold and gold leaf. Ninety per cent of the population is Buddhist, and although this is not strictly a religion but more a way of conducting yourself through this life on earth, they pay homage to statues of the Lord Buddha. He was born 543 years before Christ (the Thai calendar therefore starts from 543 BC) in India to a high ranking family, and his name was Prince Siddhartha. He had a very sheltered childhood, and when he was first allowed away from the protection of his family into his kingdom, he became very distressed to find so much misery among his subjects, so much so, that he gave up all his worldly possessions (including his wife) to live a life of contemplation and this was the beginning of his path to Enlightenment (Nirvana).

I am not sure how this was supposed to help his people, and after some years he realised this and set off travelling around his kingdom preaching a more spiritual lifestyle, and that by meditation and rejection of evil anyone could reach a state of pure happiness and enlightenment in their afterlife. Buddhism was born in an age when all Asian states were indulging in the most vicious wars with one another, and came along at the right moment for the teachings to flourish. It has succeeded in one area at least where Christianity and Islam have conspicuously failed, and that is, that no war has ever been waged in the name of the Lord Buddha.

Three of the most famous images of the Buddha are in Bangkok. The most revered is the Emerald Buddha, which is found in the Wat Phra Kaeo in the compound of the Grand Palace. Only about 30 inches high, this small statue sits on the top of a 36-foot high altar so that you can hardly see it. There are three sets of clothes for it, which are changed by the King at the beginning of each of the three seasons – the hot, the rainy and the cool.

One day, when on a visit here with some friends, I heard chanting coming from this temple. I don't know what the occasion was, but there was some sort of service in progress and the floor was packed with people chanting responses to a single monk, from a piece of paper. It was a bit like the unsung chanting of psalms in chapel when I was a boy at school, and only three notes were being used.

Visitors were being ushered behind the congregation and kept on the move, not being allowed to stand and watch, so I slipped under the rope barrier and sat down to try and fathom out what was going on. Of course I couldn't, and after ten minutes I went out and the sound of chanting went on until I was out of earshot; it made a change from the usual visit. I came away with the feeling that this magnificent temple was not just a tourist spectacle, but a living place of devotion, rather like visiting a cathedral at home while there is a service in progress.

In the neighbouring Wat Pho is the Reclining Buddha. Lying down on his right side, with his head resting on his right hand, in a viharn – or hall – all to itself, this image is as big as the Emerald Buddha is small. It is 150 feet long and 50 feet high with the soles of the feet alone being 5 feet high, and these are inlaid with mother of pearl and other precious stones depicting important Buddhist tenets.

The third is the Golden Buddha in Wat Traimet on the edge of Chinatown. In the 1950s what was thought to be an ordinary stucco statue was being moved to make way for a building project, and it was dropped by the crane. A small piece of stucco was broken off revealing something shiny underneath, and on inspection it was found to be gold. So all the stucco was removed and they found that not only was the statue covered in gold, but was solid gold – all 5 tons of it! This statue of the cross-legged Buddha seated in contemplation mode, with his right wrist resting on his right knee and his fingers almost touching the ground, was covered many years ago in order to hide its true value from Burmese invaders, and then forgotten.

Many monks spend their whole adult lives in their order, but it is common practice for young men to go into the priesthood for a few months, weeks or even days in order to gain merit for them and their families, thus ensuring a better afterlife. Merit making is very important to Buddhists in many ways. Giving to charity and putting food into monks' bowls are two of the most common ways, but building a new wat is a very extravagant method, and only done by extremely rich people. There are a number of wats in serious need of repair, but for some reason there is not so much merit to be gained in repair work as in the building of a new one.

Monks are given special seats on public transport and waiting lounges, and can always be seen at dawn walking the streets and country lanes with their begging bowls. Women, when giving money or food to monks must be careful not to touch them, as one of the strict rules of the monkhood is that they are not allowed any physical contact with members of the opposite sex. This can be difficult on a crowded bus or river taxi, both of which bump and sway along with a full load of passengers regardless of comfort or propriety!

Walking down Rama III Road one day on the way home from taking the car for a service, I heard some Thai music coming from the compound of a wat. I had to investigate and found a small orchestra, with no conductor, making the most dreadful noise. Fascinated by the repetitive nature of the notes being played apparently in the absence of any tune, I stood and watched for 15 or 20 minutes when they stopped quite suddenly, and all at the same moment!

The tune, such as it was, was being played by a man sitting in the middle of the group playing a reed instrument. On either side of him sat two men with horseshoe-shaped instruments in front of them on which there were 15 cymbals being struck more or less in unison with one another. There were two drummers, one of whom was standing, and the other sitting, using their hands to beat out the rhythm on two-sided drums. At the back, there was a bored-looking woman bashing away at three bass gongs hanging on a frame, who was dictating the rhythm, though it was not clear whether any of the others were able to recognise what it was. Finally, there were two men with boat shaped xylophones who gave a little urgency to the music with their frenetic rattling and tinkling. Seven percussion and one wind instrument were producing sounds alien to the Western ear (at least mine, anyway), but interesting for a short period. I wonder what a Thai, unfamiliar with our classics, would make of Mozart, say, or Beethoven?

There are many Holy Festival days, and the more important ones are observed with a public holiday. Visakha Bucha day in May is the day on which the Lord Buddha was born, reached Enlightenment and died, and is the most important date in the Buddhist calendar, closely followed by Makha Bucha day in February or March which is when 1,250 monks came together without any pre-arrangement to hear the Lord Buddha preach. Thawt Katin is the day each year when the laity gives new robes to the monks, and the King does this symbolically at Wat Arun, or the Temple of Dawn, on the banks of the river Choa Phraya in Bangkok. In 1999 the King was 72 years old, and as this is an auspicious date on the completion of his sixth cycle of 12 years, a great pageant was mounted as the King was rowed down the river accompanied by 52 royal barges and 2,000 naval

personnel in mediaeval dress, rowing in unis͏ͅ
stylized manner to the beat of a drum and a
chanting.

The Ploughing Ceremony, which takes place in May, is a
Brahmin rite in which two or three furrows of a public park near
the Grand Palace are turned over, and high ranking Brahmin
priests scatter grains of rice, having blessed them. The oxen
which draw the plough are then given three bowls of food to
choose to eat, and depending on which bowl they choose, the
priests are able to forecast the year's harvest, and then a free-
for-all takes place by the public to collect any seeds which have
not been buried as they are believed to be of special and holy
significance. The priests and others taking part in this ceremony
are all dressed in magnificent white and gold robes, and the
King, who is held in deep reverence by his subjects, is always in
attendance.

Two non-religious festivals take place in the spring and
autumn. In April, at the beginning of the old Thai New Year
which is at the start of the rainy season, is Songkran. This is a
four day holiday when everyone has licence to throw water over
everyone else, and celebrates the end of the dry season.
Originally the custom was to sprinkle just a few drops of water
over each other as a symbol of the precious rains returning, but
nowadays it is an orgy of water throwing in which the object is
to soak as many people to the skin as possible. Prepared, this
can be great fun, and you can give as good as you get with
water pistols and buckets. Gangs of youths roam the streets in
pick-up trucks armed with a large tank filled with water which
they throw at pedestrians, motorbikes, cars with open windows
and each other. If I found myself in the street, I had to put on a
forced smile in order not to be labelled a Grumpy Old Man! But
it is all very tiresome.

In October a really gentle and charming ceremony takes
place, called Loy Kratong. This is to celebrate the end of the
harvest and the end of the rainy season. Many parties are held

both privately and publicly, and the main constituent is that there should be some water nearby, like a lake, river or even a swimming pool. After dark everyone has a small raft made of banana wood and leaves, with a lighted candle, joss stick and a coin in it, which is launched into the water. It is a great sight to see thousands of these little kratongs floating down the river under the full moon, though if it is windy it is not nearly such a lovely sight, as the candles blow out and the waves envelop the flimsy craft.

There are quite a number of other public holidays, such as the King's birthday, the Queen's birthday and Coronation Day, which always means a long weekend if they fall between Friday and Monday, and are always welcome as an excuse to get away for three days of golf.

About the end of January or early February, the Chinese celebrate their New Year, and as there are a lot of Thais of Chinese descent, this festival is widely observed. Outside many houses and shops, papers and artefacts are burnt in small incinerators often crudely made from old oil drums, and the purpose of this is to make merit for their deceased ancestors. The paper represents money, and is bought in wads from shops beforehand, and small scale models of favourite possessions of these ancestors all go up in smoke, many of which are beautifully made, and the more beautiful, the greater the merit.

Up and down the streets and into shops and houses prance the dragon dancers. To the insistent sounds of drums and cymbals, a red dragon is draped over the heads of anything from two to fifteen young men who weave from side to side and up and down in a wave-like motion. At the head is the leader who operates the jaws of this fierce-looking apparition, which is to frighten away evil spirits along with the persistent drumming. With the larger dragons a small boy stands on the shoulders of the leader, which makes the head much taller, and thus makes it more frightening. The dragon is accompanied by men in cheerfully painted masks who appear to be teasing it into an even fiercer frenzy, while the ceaseless drumming is carried out by one man whose drum is on a little trolley being pulled by a young boy, and the cymbalists crash their way alongside him. There is great merit to be had by being a member of a troupe, so there is no shortage of volunteers to perform on the day.

While in Chinatown one day, I passed a Taoist temple from which emerged some music, which turned out to be from a tape. By the way people were moving around and chatting, it looked as though a service or ceremony was about to start, so I stayed to watch. The congregation was mainly of middle-aged women who occupied seats, while younger women sat cross-legged on the floor, and they were all dressed in white clothes. Nobody took the slightest notice of a stranger standing around while taking notes.

I was in the porchway to a shrine, and people kept on coming in to pay their respects and the air became pungent with the smoke from their smouldering incense sticks, which they planted in a bowl of sand while offering up a prayer. I was amazed to see a wizened old man come in from time to time and remove these sticks and douse them in a bucket of water - except for one, which he used to light a cigarette!

Nothing seemed to happen, and one or two people drifted away, so I did as well, none the wiser but glad to have been able to observe whatever it was.

CHAPTER 5

Social

The Thais' respect and love for the King permeates through all strata of society, and those of high birth are given the respect that they consider their due from those of lower birth, much like our perception of England up to the start of the First World War in 1914. Employers of domestic staff sometimes treat them appallingly, and they are expected to work long hours with few – if any – holidays. Buddhism takes care of this by promising that those who are down-trodden in this life will return in the next in a position of power.

Friendly at face value, Thais are not very easy to get to know well, though Bridget made some good friends amongst her pupils' parents, and I was always included in their generosity to their children's teacher, which even went on after the child had left her class. Strangers are keen that you think well of them, and are at pains to give you the answer you want to hear to any question that you may put to them. This is quite a broad generalization, and is certainly not always the case when you get to know them. On the other hand, they can be very arrogant, especially men, who will walk through a doorway allowing the door to swing in the face of whoever is behind, whether it be a stranger or their partner. It's the same with their driving, and they will change lanes with little or no warning, so that one becomes used to expecting the unexpected on the roads. This is all probably, to a large extent, due to the indulgence shown to children, who, particularly among the well-off Thais, are spoilt by their parents, nannies and maids.

Staff in shops, are on the whole, very polite to their customers, but if they don't understand your needs, or cannot be bothered to go and look for something, they simply say 'no have' with a charming smile. It is absolutely pointless in getting cross or raising your voice over anything, as this just puts up the barriers, and nothing at all happens.

I joined a small band of volunteers who spent one morning a week each answering the telephone for English-speaking people who were distressed in some way - maybe problems of a practical nature like a lost passport, or an emotional nature like an erring husband. We dealt with what we could, and we were backed up by a group of professional psychiatrists who took on what we couldn't deal with.

During training, which was largely taken up with role play to familiarize ourselves with our responses to different situations, I found myself listening to a colleague with an invented problem. Completely at a loss as to what to say, I left long silences which were interpreted as giving the 'client' time to reflect and continue talking, and for this I was held up as an example to others! Eventually I found myself in a little room with a telephone, a desk and chair and masses of mosquitoes which rather undermined my concentration on my first day, so the first thing I did at the end of this session was to buy a can of insect spray. Subsequently, with my mind on the job, I never did have to field any difficult questions.

An interesting training day out was a visit to Thanyarak Therapeutic Community. This is a drug detoxification and rehabilitation unit in Rangsit, just north of the airport. There are some 250 voluntary patients here at no cost to themselves, and many of the non-medical staff are ex-addicts themselves, who are able to empathize with their charges. We saw patients in the detox wing, which is the first stage, who were showing signs of distress and were being given small doses of certain drugs, but being voluntary, they were halfway to being cured already. Aftercare and vocational training followed, and the patients were eventually discharged to take up their lives with their families again.

This voluntary service that I had enrolled in gradually fell into disuse through lack of organization, but before it did we had a training session by a lady who spoke to us about Thai prisons, and as a prison visitor she was looking for volunteers for that job. I expressed an interest, and was soon enrolled in a small group who went to Klong Prem prison for two hours once a month.

We met on a Thursday morning, and having been relieved of our phones, sharp instruments and passports, we met prisoners on a one-to-one basis in the prison dispensary and sat round a table in a more or less civilized manner for a chat. We saw English-speaking non-Thais from the UK, other parts of Europe, Africa and Australia mainly, though our main targets were inmates from countries which had no representation in Thailand. These people saw no-one from outside from one year to the next, their families usually being too poor to visit them, and many of them were incarcerated for 30 years or more with little or no hope of seeing their home country again.

The UK, in common with many other countries, has a reciprocal agreement with Thailand that prisoners can go to their home countries having spent, I think, four years in a Thai prison, and most embassies arrange to visit their nationals once a month. But not so for countries like Ghana or Nigeria, and these were the people who appreciated our visits the most. Most of the people we saw were in for drug offences, and were aware of the risks when they agreed to carry drugs for others, and were resigned to their fate. Harsh as the sentences were, with no remission for good behaviour, they are not as harsh as Singapore where the death penalty is in place.

These monthly visits were the only break some of the prisoners had from the grinding monotony of prison life. Up at six o'clock each morning they had their rice soup breakfast at seven o'clock, and then they were 'free' until four o'clock when they had their second meal of the day – more rice soup – then lock-up at 6 o/c in the evening for a further 12 hours in their cells. Money is everything, from buying favours from the guards (like turning a blind eye to the television that the family has brought in) to buying food at the shop. Only Thai prisoners are allowed to work, and they are often seen on the streets of Bangkok performing the most unpleasant jobs like cleaning out the drains in the street after a storm.

This all came to an abrupt end when one day a group of prisoners from another prison broke out taking the governor as hostage. They had somehow acquired a gun, stolen a prison truck and disappeared off in the direction of Burma, but they were caught near Kanchanaburi where there was a shoot-out and all were killed, including the governor. The authorities immediately stopped our visits for about a year, and though we did get back, it was not to the round table in the dispensary, but we had to join visiting relatives and shout across an eight-foot gap with warders prowling up and down this alleyway. We were separated by thick wire netting to prevent any contact and I had the greatest difficulty hearing what was said as the noise was horrendous. I really couldn't cope with this, so I regretfully gave this job up.

CHAPTER 6

A Brush with Royalty

The princess Royal, Her Highness Maha Chakri Sirindorn, is the daughter of His Majesty the King of Thailand, and she is a dedicated supporter of the charities of which she is a patron. One of these charities is a school for poor children, way up in the hills near the Burmese border called Baan Tam Hin in the village of Suang Phueung, and Shrewsbury School, where Bridget was now a teacher, had raised some money for them.

The Princess was due to make one of her regular visits there on December 14th 2004, and I was asked if I would like to present a cheque to her on behalf of the School. Of course I would! Whether members of staff were too busy to go (the next day was the last day of term) or that they knew I had a decent suit, I don't know, but I was very happy to take this opportunity of doing a very "Thai" thing.

I presented myself to a Thai parent, who was organising this trip to the hills early in the morning and we took mini buses to Chitralada School, where we met up with more children who were also making a presentation to the Princess. My early start came to nothing really, as by the time we stocked up with snacks, sweets and fizzy drinks for the journey, we didn't leave Bangkok until about ten o'clock.

The minibuses were not that comfortable, and although I had plenty of room on the back seat on my own, the shock absorbers on the back axle were not in the prime of youth. As we progressed into the hinterland, the roads got worse, and so did the bumps.

At midday we stopped in a little village where lunch had been pre-arranged in an open sala under a bamboo roof, and there we consumed a tasty rice dish and drank water. It was stiflingly hot as there was not a hint of a breeze, and although I had taken my jacket off, I was still freely perspiring in my long sleeve shirt and tie.

Eventually we made our way to the school, but now with a police escort as there was massive security in the area, and were shown around the premises, with classrooms about 10 ft by 10 ft. Elderly computers were around, as these were given to the school by firms who were upgrading their business equipment, and they were immensely proud of their library which contained about 1,000 books, many of which were text books. This made me realise just how lucky our children are and what a difference even a small contribution would make to a school here.

The playground was a flattish area in front of the school on which a takraw court was marked out in the dust. This is a game played with a small ball made of woven basket-work (it doesn't bounce) which is kept in the air, using the feet only, by a team of three on each side of a badminton net. It is played widely in Thailand as the surface of the playing area is not important.

And then it was just rather a lot of hanging about. There were masses of police and army of all ranks in evidence, and also a large number of high ranking civilians wearing their very smart military-style white suits with black shoes. On top of all this – or perhaps I should say below – were the TV crews and vans with satellite dishes, all ready to film and televise the progress of the Princess. There was no signal on my phone in this remote area, and so there were many aerials extending high into the sky for the security chiefs to keep in touch with one another.

At long last at about three o'clock we heard the chopping of a helicopter which landed a short distance away – the playground would have been far too dusty – and very soon the Princess swept up the road in a convoy of several Mercedes cars. She was greeted by the head teacher and various officials before heading off on a tour of the school. She keeps careful notes of all her visits, and if she recommends something in one visit, she expects it to be implemented in the next. This keeps everyone on their toes, and it also underlines the real interest that she takes in all her charities.

I had been standing in line in the library with the people I had come with for about an hour before the Princess got to us for the presentations, and I had been rehearsed in the procedure I must adopt when it was my turn. I was given a paan – a sort of gilded cake stand – on which I put the envelope containing the cheque. When the Princess got to me I was to bow, reach forward with the paan, bow again, and when she had taken the offering, reach back and bow for a third time, and that I was not to look at her. This all went off very well – so I was told – then she was gone with her entourage, and the helicopter was no more than a buzz in the distance.

The children, who had been good all day, were allowed to let off a little steam. We had brought little presents for them, like soap, toothbrushes, sweets, notebooks and pencils, which we handed out, but the best things were several footballs which went down very well.

The whole day, although very wearisome in the heat, was most rewarding, and it underlined for me the vast chasm there is here between the rich and the poor, the wealth being in the cities and poverty in the countryside.

CHAPTER 7

Holidays and Golf

As well as going abroad when we could, we took several long weekends at the seaside and playing golf. One of our favourite destinations was Hua Hin, which is about two hours south of Bangkok on the west coast of the Gulf of Siam. There are some lovely sandy beaches away from the centre which are not at all crowded, though there is often a problem with jellyfish in the sea, but as all hotels have their own swimming pools this did not worry us too much.

Nearby there are several very good golf courses, and the one we went to most was the Majestic Creek, about half an hour away, and we usually stayed at the Majestic Beach Resort, which was associated with the golf course. It was built in a U-shape with the pool in the middle and steps on to the beach, and we used to enjoy an early morning walk before breakfast in the sunshine, paddling in the warm water. We went here about twice a year, and I always had the same caddy who was a young man who spoke fairly good English; he himself played off a handicap of eight. It must have been very painful for him to watch me hit the ball, but he was always cheerful, and gave me some useful coaching. (The only time he failed me was when I paid him after a game on Saturday, and he was completely unfit on Sunday morning. Thereafter, I paid him at the end of the weekend!)

A visit has to be made to the old Railway Hotel, now the Sofitel, which has extensive gardens with one area devoted to topiary which is lit up at night. There are three pools, outdoor terraces for food and drink, a private beach and masses of history. Built when the railway first arrived in Hua Hin in the 1800s, it was the seaside home of the King until he built his own palace some two or three miles away. It is quite sumptuous and expensive even by UK standards, but 'Happy Hour' cocktails between five and six o'clock in the evening are not to be missed. There are some lovely restaurants in town to suit all wallets and tastes. Italian, German, English (breakfasts mainly), Thai and other Asian cuisine abound, and the seafood restaurants, built out on piers over the sea, offer the most delicious dishes of the freshest fish you could imagine. The bars in the town are always very busy, and the atmosphere invariably friendly.

On the east side of the Gulf, more or less opposite Hua Hin, is the town of Pattaya. A fishing village in the 1960s, it was developed as a 'rest and recreation' resort for US troops during the Vietnam war in the 1970s. It is so completely different from Hua Hin, and the atmosphere is definitely seedy, as all sorts of facilities are available here including virtually any sexual deviation that can be imagined – and probably many that can't! The bars advertise themselves with garish lights which leave little to the imagination of the delights to be found inside, and when walking round the town I kept my hand firmly on my wallet, as I have had my pocket picked once in Bangkok, and didn't want that experience again. There are, however, some lovely golf courses around, and many ex-pats retire to the area, and spend their days playing golf in the most delightful of surroundings where the sun (nearly) always shines, it is never cold and when it rains, it usually only lasts for half an hour or so. Idyllic!

For non-golfing holidays, there are several islands around the coast of Thailand which are well worth a visit. Koh (island) Samui, Koh Samet, and Koh Chang, to mention just three, are in the Gulf of Siam and Koh Phuket is in the Anderman Sea which we visited just after the tsunami of 2004. We spent a few days by the sea on Koh Phi Phi, which is about two hours from Phuket by ferry, and we arrived in lovely calm conditions and swam in the clearest of seas with fish and coral, but during our first night a fierce storm blew up which disturbed the sea bed to such an extent that we were unable to see the bottom again. The ferry ride out was lovely, but the return trip was awful, as a huge swell on the surface as a result of the storm made many people sick, and we were slightly apprehensive as to whether the craft was stable anyway. However, we made it OK! This island was overrun by the tsunami wave four years later.

Three hours north of Bangkok, near Saraburi, we often went to Sir James' Lodge, another delightful golf course and resort amongst the hills. Having played golf with our society for three days during the school holidays, we stayed on for a couple of nights on one occasion to explore the countryside. We didn't have the usual frantic run back to Bangkok on Sunday night for one thing, and we were able to play golf on an empty course on Monday, swim in the pool and visit a decent restaurant nearby. And next day we drove around some very rural roads looking at the farming, and eating at roadside stalls for a most relaxing day.

Nearby is Khao Yai National Park which we visited with a group from the British Club for a weekend on a non-golfing break. We walked through forest and jungle paths enjoying the wildlife which was really only monkeys, although there is reputed to be a tiger lurking about in the area. There are also wild elephants, but we did not see any of these on this trip. It had been raining, and the forest floor was quite wet and we were attacked by leeches. These little slug-like creatures of about two inches in length or less quickly attached themselves to your shoe and started creeping up towards your skin. Having been warned, we were very wary of them and flicked them away as soon as we saw them, but one member of the party got herself bitten quite badly as she was wearing only flip-flops on her feet, and she had no chance against these little critters. But fancy wearing this sort of footwear on a jungle walk anyway! The only way to get rid of them is by burning them with a cigarette or a lighter, but this is really not a lot of help to a non-smoker.

About four hours away from Bangkok to the south-east is the pretty little town of Chantaburi in the heart of the rambutan growing area and not far from the Cambodian border. We used to go here about once a year and spend a long weekend on Soi Dao Highland Golf Course. Hilly, picturesque and always in good condition, it was one of our favourites, and being that far from Bangkok it was never as crowded as the courses nearer home, which are always so congested at weekends. The journey was a bit tiresome, though, as only the first quarter was on the expressway, and as we drew nearer our destination the traffic always seemed to build up.

On one occasion we were brought to a standstill in two lanes of traffic which slowly made its way over a road covered in red stains. We could only think that there had been a horrific accident here earlier, but it turned out that it was the middle of the rambutan harvest, and growers were selling their produce on the road side and the staining was the inevitable result of the fruits spilling from their containers and being squashed! One of the memorable things about this course had nothing to do with golf: on the tenth fairway we came across a scorpion scampering across the grass, which stopped to look at us when we approached. Bridget took out a six-iron and gently touched its tail which it immediately flicked into a menacing position over its body. We of course allowed it to take itself off into the undergrowth quite safely, but it is the only time I have ever seen one in the wild.

Golf is a very popular game, especially among the wealthier citizens, although green fees are not high by UK standards. Four-and-a-half-hour rounds are normal at weekends, while five and even six hour rounds are not uncommon. The trouble is that many people play five and six-ball games which can be so slow, and if you get behind a group who seem to be unaware of the etiquette having lost ground on the game in front, it can be very frustrating. Every four to six holes there is a drinks hut, and it is essential to keep your liquids topped up in the heat, so the sensible golfers take on water. Others take on beer which after a while makes a bad shot seem less bad, and can even reduce the frustration of a slow round! Noodle dishes are often available at these stops, and it can be a great annoyance to see the five-ball in front get up to go to the next tee after food, just as you leave the green. So you have to stop whether you wanted to or not.

This all sounds a very negative approach, but I really enjoyed my golf in Thailand, playing in the hot sunshine most of the time, just wearing shorts and a shirt all year round. Mind you, when there was a storm the rain came down in stair rods, and if there was a danger of lightning, a hooter was sounded and everyone was obliged to leave the course and seek shelter in one of the drinks huts. Now that can become very convivial! Having got wet, though, when the sun came out again you quickly got dry, and steam was to be seen rising off golfers' clothes all around – but shoes remained soggy, which was a little bit unpleasant. Weekday golf was much less stressful, and I was lucky enough to be able to do this at least once a week.

Generally speaking, when we first got to Thailand and started going on weekend trips with the British Club, it was inexpensive and it could be said that this was something that you could not afford to miss. For a double room with breakfast for two nights and for two rounds of golf each, we paid about 100 to 150 pounds for the weekend – and that is only 50 to 75 pounds each! Some London clubs charge twice as much as this for a single round, and other prestigious clubs are not far behind. When we left, prices had gone up somewhat, but were still only 150 to 200 pounds.

We went on a short golfing holiday to Chiang Rai in 2004 with the British Club. Being a domestic flight, Bridget had no trouble with the immigration authorities at the airport over her unpaid taxes from 1999 and 2000 (the result of a misunderstanding by the school's accountants of her liabilities Which was eventually resolved in 2004), so it was a much less stressful flight than we have had lately.

Being in the north, it is a little cooler than Bangkok, and the weather was ideal for golf and we enjoyed the course at Santaburi which was rather like an English parkland course, though it was inadvisable to go looking for your ball in the trees, or even deep rough, on account of the snakes. Waterford Valley was similar, and we really enjoyed the quiet surroundings in this very rural part of Thailand – in fact I missed one afternoon of golf so that I could sit on the balcony of our chalet-style room overlooking the wooded valley and lake.

The restaurant of this resort left a lot to be desired, but we made up for it with our own conviviality, though at breakfast on the second day, I asked for some toast to put under my fried egg. "Solly sir, no toa'." (The Thais tend to mix up their 'l's and r's, and do not pronounce their final consonants in their own language) "Well then, could I have some bread, please?" "Solly sir, no blea', that why no toa'" Silly me!

Nevertheless, it was a great few days away.

CHAPTER 8

An Incident at the British Club

We joined the British Club soon after we arrived in order to play golf with their golf section, which consisted of about 30 regular playing members. In some ways quite an old fashioned ex-pat club that I imagine can be found in many parts of the world, it suited our needs quite well, and gave us a useful base which was not very far from home. The staff were always friendly, and we took part in some of the functions which they organised like the Christmas Ball that took place outside on the lawn each year, or the boat trip with dinner on New Year's Eve, which always ended up with a good view of the fantastic firework displays put on by two or three of the five-star hotels on the river.

I was researching something else amongst their records (I was treasurer of the golf section for four years), and I came across an item relating to the application for membership of a prospective member, and maybe I have embellished this account to a certain degree, but I wrote the following piece which was printed in the monthly magazine.

"The members recoiled in horror. They were struck dumb, and it seemed that no one knew what to do or say next.

The committee had been in existence for about 50 or 60 years, and some thought the original members were still on it.

Since its inception, there had been two world wars, and many other world shattering events, but not even having the enemy in the second war take over their premises was able to shock the members as much as this.

There before them appeared a young man of impeccable credentials, who was applying for membership. His sponsors stood by his side and, to give them their due, were somewhat embarrassed by the situation, but there was nothing they could do about it now: The Applicant Was Not Wearing a Tie! Had he been trouser-less, it could not have caused more concern, but he was tie-less, and the sight of his uncovered neck had completely thrown the committee into disarray. So they immediately went into discussion in camera, and emerged after what seemed like several months to inform the young man that his application was denied, with no reasons given for their decision."

This account is a fanciful version of an incident which took place in the British Club in the 1960s or 1970s. Could it happen today, in the twenty-first century? Certainly not, but it does give an insight into what our forefathers considered to be important.

This is not meant to be a criticism of them, but it made me wonder what standards of behaviour which we accept as normal today will be laughed at as incredible in 2050? Not wearing shorts in the Churchill Bar after 6 pm seems reasonable to me, as is not wearing sweaty sports gear at any time, but what will they think 50 years hence?

There are many clubs in the UK where it is obligatory to wear a jacket and a tie, and you do not have to be a member of a club of whose rules you disapprove, but in those days expatriates were expected to be members of both the British Club and the Royal Bangkok Sports Club, so they had no choice other than to abide by the rules as they found them.

Things have changed, moved on. In these days of informal dress, jeans, which were designed as tough working trousers, and trainers for sport, are now an acceptable form of dress in all walks of life. Yesterday's informal dress over the ages becomes tomorrow's formal attire, and this is a continuing process, which is fine as long as manners are preserved, as they are not negotiable.

Smartness is in the eye of the beholder, and one should dress in a manner which does not offend others. Clean T-shirts and jeans without holes will become acceptable more and more on semi-formal occasions, but a sleeveless singlet is, I hope, a long way off! A tie has been described as giving the wearer a spurious air of respectability, while performing no useful purpose. Well, maybe, but does the absence of one make a man a vagrant?

Having said all this, we found the club to be quite a convivial place though the general committee had a very difficult job trying to keep all factions of the membership happy with their plans. There was always someone who was willing to articulate objections to whatever they proposed, while being unwilling to stand for the committee themselves.I suppose most clubs suffer from this, and the British Club is no exception.

CHAPTER 9

Memorable meals

Bangkok has a plethora of excellent restaurants, and except for the five-star hotels, by and large four can eat for the price of one in the UK. We went to Lord Jim's restaurant in the Oriental Hotel for Christmas lunch on three or four occasions, where we had the most sumptuous buffet meal for about 25 pounds. We could help ourselves to prawns, oysters, mussels, crab, lobster, smoked salmon and many other sea foods. Cold meats, quails eggs and avocado – you name it, they had it – all accompanied with salads of all sorts. The main courses were equally varied and delicious, with turkey, beef, lamb, pork and ham and whatever trimmings that you fancied, all for Europeans. Thai, Chinese and Indian cuisine was there as well, to cater for all tastes.

And then the sweets, from Christmas pudding and fruits to creme brulee and ice cream, all had to be tasted, though by this time there was not a lot of room! Sitting on the terrace with coffee afterwards in one of the top ten hotels in the world in the warm afternoon sunshine overlooking the Chao Phraya river, is an amazing end to Christmas Day in the tropics.

Trader Vic's restaurant at the Marriott Riverside Hotel was certainly our favourite destination for a Sunday lunch. We used to go there in a party of six to ten people, and sat outside on the terrace overlooking the river and the spectacular concrete

Krungthep Bridge. From midday until three o'clock for about 20 pounds we were able to indulge ourselves in a very similar buffet meal as at Lord Jim's, but with 'free flow' booze. Red wine, white wine, beer or cocktails kept on coming to the table, and that was as well as our very favourite starter – oyster cocktails. These were made with a shot of vodka being poured over an oyster, with a dash of worcester sauce and green tabasco, and then slugged back in one! Unbelievable.

In addition to the buffet, there were little stalls set up where chefs cooked succulent fillet steaks for you, barbequed sausages or fish, and foie gras with bacon. You had to watch the time, though, as at three o'clock precisely the 'free flow' drinks dried up. We made the mistake of ordering another litre of house wine after this time on our first visit there, which cost an arm and a leg, so never again!

We never drove to this place and usually took a taxi to Thaksin Bridge and caught one of the two shuttle boats which spent the day ferrying the hotel guests to and from the main part of Bangkok. We returned the same way, usually a little the worse for wear, and it was at about four o'clock in the afternoon on one of these trips that one of my golfing partners declared that I was his "besh fren'," and promptly fell over! On another occasion, Bridget, along with Karen (another golfing friend) and a school colleague, stripped off to their bras and pants and took a dip in the hotel swimming pool! No one seemed to mind, or at least were too polite to comment.

Perched high above Bangkok on about the seventieth floor in the open air is Vertigo Restaurant in the Banyan Tree Hotel. Aptly named, you could look over the edge straight down on to the street below. Closed for rain and high winds, it is a most spectacular place to eat, but the view of the city below and the stars above, without the layer of pollution, is probably more memorable than the meal.

On Sunday afternoons at the Shangri La Hotel, another hotel in Bangkok in the top ten in the world, there is a tea dance. A quintet in one corner of the lounge scraped and sawed away in strict tempo for dancers to perform the quickstep, foxtrot, tango and waltz and other long-forgotten steps. Many of them were performing in the most professional manner, and once or twice I had the urge to stomp around with Bridget, though I felt very inadequate amongst the regulars gliding around the floor. Many of the dancers were highly made-up women of more mature years with much younger men, who we were told were teaching professionals hired for the afternoon.

That was the 'entertainment', and the buffet tea that we had for about seven or eight pounds was enough for one day's intake of food. Smoked salmon, cheese, cold meats and salads along with spicy Thai dishes were all there, with peking duck being cooked as required. Sweets and puddings of the richest and most fattening sorts followed, including a chocolate fountain in which you held a small piece of fruit on a cocktail stick that got covered in the chocolate, and this all went down with a wide choice of teas or coffee. I must say, this was a serious binge session, and was only a very occasional outing.

I held my seventieth birthday party at Ban Chiang restaurant, where we went several times. An old house, built on several levels with small rooms and converted into a restaurant, it has a charming atmosphere and very welcoming staff. The foods are brought to the table in bowls so that we could help ourselves to each dish, Thai style, and eat with chopsticks. Good food, not too spicy, accompanied by reasonably priced wine made us take our guests here perhaps more than anywhere else. I ordered ten set meals for four for about 30 guests at my party, and it was all gobbled up, and I had to keep on ordering more wine to keep up with them! The occasion was great, and the best bit was the bill, which was a fraction of my sixtieth birthday party at Chilston Park in Kent!

Michel, the proprietor of Indigo, a French restaurant in Convent Road, invited us along with about 20 other people for a gourmet meal to introduce a new chef. We knew four of the others from the British Club and the rest were French, all of whom spoke good English, and we sat at two large tables and waited for a pre-arranged meal to be served.

We started with a mouth-watering bouchon of caviar and cheese wrapped in the shortest of pastry, followed by haddock in new potatoes accompanied by a Sancerre. All too delicious, with portions not too large. Small medallions of roast saddle of lamb followed, which melted in my mouth, with mashed potatoes and basil, making them green. This went down with a lovely Rhone wine.

Finally, and almost too much, was a coffee tart with whipped cream, and with that we were given a 25-year-old brandy. This was nectar, and I had to have more than one glass even though I am not normally very fond of brandy. It was an evening of a great gastronomic experience and conviviality which was well worth the 25 pounds each that we paid. Michel held a raffle at the end, and one of Bridget's teacher colleagues won a magnum of the red wine we had been drinking, which she brought up to our flat the following week, and so we lived a part of the evening again.

We came here many times, and they had a courtyard with tables under umbrellas, which was quiet and friendly and much preferable to sitting inside, which we obviously had to do when it was wet.

Another French restaurant, Le Boucheron, is tucked away among the seedy bars of Patpong, and seats about 20 to 24 people at most. 'Le patron' is a large affable Frenchman whose chief idea in life seems to be to pour out drinks for his customers, charging for them on a rather haphazard basis. At the end of an amazing meal of moules, steaks, fish and so on, with an excellent but inexpensive house wine, he comes round with a bottle of calvados just to make sure that you'll go back! The trouble is that you can never get in on the spur of the moment, and for a weekend you have to book at least two weeks in advance.

The Ban Klang Nam is a very Thai fish restaurant which is at the end of a scruffy little side road off Rama III Road, on the waterfront of the river. When we first went there the only menu was in Thai, and the staff had to interpret in halting English, but this changed as it became better known amongst the ex-pat community. Part of the restaurant sits on piles over the water, and part is on an old barge moored alongside. The floor of the whole place is made of rather uneven wooden planking, and a breeze blows through sides, as there are no walls. It is nice to sit at a table by the rails on the edge, but if it rains there is no protection, and you simply get very wet! If it rains very hard, the side road fills up with flood water, and you have to drive through a foot of water to get home, and if it rains very, very hard, the car park floods as well.

The food is excellent, and you can choose your fish from the tanks by the entrance and it is all cooked for you as required, and served with different sorts of rice. Here you can buy beer or bring your own wine, and one of the attractions of this place is its total lack of any pretensions. The bare wooden tables were always kept clean, the service quick and friendly, and the place was always full and very good value.

On one lunchtime visit, I was idly watching a small barge with a JCB on board slowly making its way upstream. It had no motor, and the JCB appeared to be dredging the river bed, but not bringing anything up, and it dawned on me as it got nearer that it was using its digger arm as a method of propulsion. It moored nearby, and the driver got out and walked away – but what an ingenious way to get along.

At the end of the street where our apartments were was a roadside café which we called The Shack. Just a corrugated tin roof over about 50 or so plastic tables, this place turned over a huge number of meals during an evening, and was always full. The gas and charcoal cookers kept going all night (almost), turning out the simplest dishes of fish, chicken or other meats, with lots of rice, and I don't think we ever paid more than about

50p each. I usually ordered the cheap Thai Mekong whisky, as I am not fond of the ice cold fizzy lagers you get here; this goes down very well with coca cola.

One night in September 2001 we were just finishing a meal there and were about to go home, when the heavens opened and chucked down the rain so heavily that we decided to buy another small bottle of whisky and wait half an hour for the storm to blow over. We got home at about 9 p.m. and turned on the television to see the news before going to bed. CNN was on the air, and there were pictures of smoke billowing from one of the WTC towers in New York, which is 12 hours behind Bangkok. It was September 11th, and the commentators thought that a plane had crashed out of control into the tower – that is until another one crashed into the other tower.

We sat there transfixed at the unfolding horror of this terrorist outrage in the centre of New York. We watched unbelievingly as the flames engulfed the towers until they eventually collapsed, killing what was thought to be at the time upwards of 6,000 people. And this was all live on TV. Like remembering where you were when, say, President Kennedy was assassinated, I shall always remember where I was on the night of 9/11.

New Year's Eve is an important secular holiday in Thailand, and we usually signed up for a party on a boat organised by the British Club. We enjoyed a buffet meal on board while the boat steamed up and down the river with a party of over 100 people becoming more and more convivial, as the drinks were included up until midnight. After three hours of this, we arrived back at Sathorn Bridge which is adjacent to both the Shangri La and the Oriental hotels, where we moored mid-stream along with many other boats – in fact there were so many, you could almost walk across the river on them!

From here we watched the most fantastic firework displays put on by the three major hotels in the area, which included the Peninsular Hotel, lasting 15 to 20 minutes. With the sky above on fire, and thousands of coloured sparks cascading hither and thither and with the constant bangs, one would have thought we were in a war zone. Maybe New Year's Eve would be a good time to invade the city or start a revolution! On the night of 1999/2000, a laser beam was focused on the side of the Oriental hotel, and the seconds were counted down to the new millennium and this was followed by the best display ever, lasting at least half an hour.

Peter Bond, another golfing friend, organised three safari dinners on three separate occasions while we were in Bangkok, which consisted of having different courses in different locations in a hotel. The best one was at the Sheraton Grand, where we started by whizzing up about 50 or 60 floors to the roof. Here we were served with the most succulent nibbles including smoked salmon on rye bread, and ducks liver cooked (as required) in brandy, which absolutely melted in my mouth, but was really so filling and fattening! Accompanied by ad lib champagne (or whisky, gin, beer or anything else for that matter), we gasped at the unbelievable sight below of Bangkok at night. About eight feet below was the roof of the next floor, so that was as far as you could go, though the six inch (yes, six inch!) parapet did not really offer much protection from even that short fall!

On the way to the main course by the swimming pool, we hurtled down (by lift) to the basement into the main control room for all the air con, TV and video machines, for asparagus and freshly cooked prawns, with more champagne. A long table had been set up by the pool, with white linen and sparkling cutlery and glassware, and we sat down to medallions of lamb as tender as I have ever had. It was nouvelle cuisine, and so there was more plate than meat, but the mushroom flan and mashed potatoes were a great complement to the dish. Served with an exquisite chilled claret, I could happily have finished here!

Dessert, coffee and liqueurs were served in room 1010, which with its own small garden and pool, was totally out of sight of any part of the hotel, and it was said to cost in the region of US$ 1,000 per night. How the other half live!

On another occasion we went to the Regent (now the Four Seasons) Hotel, and started in a public room. Being election day, no alcohol can be consumed in public (not really an inspired day on which to organise such an event!), so we had soft cocktails while we sampled the most delectable pieces of bite-sized pizza in Biscotti's restaurant. From here we went into a private room where we were taught how to make a simple Japanese dish by a sushi chef, and I found that I was not very adept at rolling the pastry for this dish, but the best part here was the saki we were given to taste. Two large men dressed as sumo wrestlers brought round five different bottles for us to try, and I must say that after a while, I couldn't really distinguish one from another!

The main course by the pool was barbequed beef, lamb, pork and prawns all cooked to perfection, and the accompanying wines were as good. From there we were taken to the bowels of the hotel into the deep freeze, where we were given some thick clothes to wear. We sat at tables and chairs made of ice at –10°C, and were served up with the most delicious ice cream with liqueurs in a spooky atmosphere lit with candles, and the staff dressed up as monks with their hoods covering their heads and faces.

On the third occasion, we went to the Marriott Riverside (in which Trader Vic's is situated) and again started on the roof. With the main course of barbequed fillet steak, we were invited by the chefs to help cook the stir fried vegetables in woks. This we did, with varying degrees of success in the art of tossing the contents and catching them in the wok rather than on the floor! The wine kept on coming, and finally in the kitchens we were given ice cream which was so delicious that I completely lost track of what was in it by the time I had finished this alcoholic dish.

These three outings were not cheap by Bangkok standards so it was not something we wanted to do too often, but the experience of being served up with gourmet food and wine in the most unusual and unlikely places by the most attentive staff was something neither of us would have missed.

CHAPTER 10

Fruits and Plants

Thailand is full of exotic fruits, many of which are familiar to us in the U K, but seeing them growing was a real experience. There are several different varieties of mango and although in modern commercial plantations they are grown on small trees no taller than a man can reach, there are plenty of magnificent old trees of up to 15 metres in height, on which hang the pendulous fruits.

In certain areas, fields of pineapple stretch for miles. Fruits grow vertically from ground level amongst spiky leaves, and each plant lasts no more than four or five years. On the many fresh fruit vendors stalls in Bangkok, this fruit is always available, and it is quite an education to watch them being sliced up. First a v-shaped spiral is cut through the skin to extract the rather chewy bits, and then the rest of the skin is peeled off. The flesh is cut lengthways from the inedible core and chopped into bite-sized pieces, and popped into a polythene bag with a small stick – all for 10 baht or about 15p. And this is all done in the twinkling of an eye, and is very welcome in the middle of a hot day. Mangoes and watermelon are always available on these stalls as well, as are guava and papaya.

Durian is a fruit that I did not see growing, but it has the distinction of being banned from many public places on account of its disgusting smell! It is worth, however, persevering with it as the flavour is perfectly acceptable, though the texture is not all that brilliant. Papaya, or paw paw, come in long pendulous shapes and grow rather like mangoes on trees, but on much smaller ones.

Mangosteen are purple golf-ball-sized fruits enclosing several ivory coloured segments, not unlike small tangerines. Rambutan, which grow in clusters on the branches of quite large trees, are also golf-ball-sized; they are a dull red in colour, the husk being covered in soft spiky hairs about half an inch long. Inside is a single oval of flesh with a large nut inside which is easily separated. Guava is an apple-sized fruit with a rough skin. It has seeds inside which make the texture gritty, and has little flavour.

Pomelo is a citrus fruit which is rather like a large grapefruit to look at, but the flesh is infinitely sweeter, and this we consumed in quantities. I tried to peel one once, but it is so cheap to buy them ready sectioned, that the trouble and difficulty of doing it was not worth while. Bananas are everywhere, in all sizes from three inches to over a foot long. The bunches, or hands, grow from a long pendulous flower (which is also edible) on large-leaved trees. These leaves are used extensively in cooking to wrap up hot and cold foods, and also as a mat on a plate. Pandanas leaves are also used a great deal in cooking, and give a unique flavour to the food which is wrapped in them. They grow in profusion in the wild, and are also cultivated.

Water (Rose) apples or champoo are small pear-shaped fruits which are very crisp and juicy, though with not a great deal of flavour,; these grow on large trees, many of which overhang pavements, providing shade in the streets, from private gardens. Water melons look just like very large marrows, and grow the same way. These very juicy fruits are found ready to eat on the street fruit stalls and have absolutely no food value at all, but are extremely welcome on a hot dusty day in the city.

Coconuts, when ripe, can fall at any moment, and walking under these palm trees at harvest time is a hazardous thing to do! The milk is used in cooking and can be drunk, the sap of the flowers is made into alcohol and the interior pulp is grated and eaten by itself and used to decorate cakes. The hairy outside is used in the making of ropes, and the leaves are used as roofing material. The fruits of the sugar palm are used to make margarine and oil, and the trees are distinctive by being up to 20 or 25 metres high with a small bunch of leaves on the top of a bare trunk. For harvesting the bunches of small nuts, a rickety wooden ladder is fixed to the stem up which the picker scampers with no apparent fear. Not for me!

Seeing the cashew nut growing was a surprise in that the nut itself grows out of the eye of a small pear shaped fruit, which is itself edible. In fact what is called the 'nut' is the fruit, and the 'fruit' is the swollen stem. Coffee grows in clusters of small red berries on bushes, and there are two beans in each berry. It is often grown as a decorative plant as well, and if harvested in the garden, you need 20 beans per cup of coffee. Groundnuts, as we saw in Burma, grow on the roots of the plants underground, and ginger also is obtained from the rhizomes of plants, also underground.

Rice is grown almost anywhere that is flat, which means that the Central Plain around Bangkok is covered in paddy fields. It is usual to produce two crops a year grown from seed, but if seedlings are planted in the flooded fields, three crops can be grown and often are. Thailand is a major producer of rice, and exports much of it around the world.

Opium is grown legally and illegally because the product of the plant is used in small quantities to alleviate pain, while abuse causes short-term relief but long-term suffering. Bamboo is a plant seen in clumps all over the place. Fast growing, it is said that it has over 1,000 uses, and one of the scariest is seeing it used as scaffolding, tied together with string, on the tallest of buildings. Tall rubber trees planted some six or eight feet apart in neat rows all have a little cup attached to the trunk into which drains latex from incisions made in the bark. With little light penetrating through to the ground, these plantations appear rather foreboding.

There are many different palm trees; one of the most spectacular is the Traveller's Palm which grows to a height of 10 to 15 meters with leaves radiating from a central stem in a regular fan shape. It is said that in the base of the leaf sheaths water collects, and this is what gives it its name, as it can be used by weary or even desperate travellers. Many formal gardens contain this plant which looks so dramatic on its own, with a few large rocks or stones at its base. Teak trees are majestic, growing up to 50 metres high, quite straight. They are used extensively to make furniture, as not only is the wood fairly easy to work, but the oil in it is believed to keep it free of fungi and termites.

CHAPTER 11

China October 1999

My overall impression of China is the sheer number of people who live there. It was my first and my last impression. One has known since schooldays that about one fifth of the world's population is Chinese, but to see what looked like all of them on bicycles in Beijing at once, was an amazing sight.

We found that the people were not very courteous – at least to us. There were seven of us, four colleagues from school and Edward, and perhaps we were seen as capitalist enemies of the State, and as such merited no courtesy. Whatever it was, change was slapped down on a shop counter without a smile or even a glance on many occasions. The receptionists in two of the hotels we stayed in did not seem to care whether we stayed or not, and in fact in one of them we had to pay for each night in advance. We had booked four nights at this hotel, and we arrived with only 100 Yuan notes in our pockets and the room rate was 272 Yuan per night, and the miserable elderly receptionist would only accept the correct money as she had no change. She would not accept 300 Yuan and carry forward 28 until the next day, and so we had an impasse. Bureaucracy Rules OK! This was resolved by a kindly fellow guest who had a pocket full of change, and was also probably embarrassed by the receptionist's hostility to foreign guests. So we got our key cards and a good night's sleep, and after the following day in the city, we went back to our rooms to find that the cards had been blocked and we had to go through the whole performance of paying exactly for one more night all over again.

That was in Beijing, but in other places we found the Chinese very friendly, for example in the Muslim Quarter of Xi'an, and maybe this was because we were potential (and rich) customers for their merchandise. We took an evening walk in this area, where the street stalls were selling cooked and uncooked foods, as well as many artifacts in a street market. We stopped by a stall selling calligraphy pens, and the owner took a great deal of trouble in showing us how to hold and use them, and while talking to him we somehow acquired a charming English speaking young girl who took us to an art studio. She introduced us to a painter and an art teacher and a studio full of paintings and drawings of all sorts, and before we bought a wall hanging of about five feet by eighteen inches, we had a fascinating hour looking through their work.

The studio was in a hutong, and we walked, I must admit rather nervously, up this extremely narrow and dark alleyway, which then opened up on to a tiny and charming courtyard. Although it could have only had the merest glimpse of the sun at noonday, it was full of pots of the most colourful flowers, and with mediaeval plaques let into the plaster on the walls and a bridge over the hutong connecting the upper floors, one felt as though one had gone back in time by at least 100 years.

The Chinese appear to be quite happy to be told what to do – at least the older people do, who swapped one despotic regime for another in 1949. The young who are the product of the one-child family policy are spoilt and appear arrogant in public, and though these days the authorities turn a blind eye to this policy, they may be a force to reckon with in later years. We did not see this going on, but police vans tour Tiananmen Square and in a none too discreet manner pick up protesting members of the Falun Gong, a sect which opposes government religious policies, and take them off to God knows where, a bit like stray dogs.

We saw few motorbikes, and more cars than I expected. There are many thousands of bicycles, and they are the kings of the road, having their own carriageway, not always in the gutter either. They are so sure of their rights that they pedal across the road at intersections with an apparent death wish, but are respected completely by cars, and we saw no accidents. There are masses of inexpensive taxis and the drivers are all caged in to their seats, which suggest that crime has not been eliminated from The People's Republic of China. We did see one inconsequential accident where a motorbike skidded onto its side. He was trying to avoid a man walking across the street with some six-foot lengths of timber on his shoulder, who had no idea of the trouble he had caused, and just kept on walking - quite comical, really. In Xi'an we saw two men wrestling and apparently trying to knock hell out of one another, which ended peacefully. There was a terrific crack as they fell on the pavement, and it sounded as if at least one of them had broken his head open, but they helped one another up, dusted themselves off and separated peacefully.

That was in Xi'an, and in Guilin we were walking round the edges of the centre of the city where it was a little less antiseptic, looking at older homes and street markets. We came across an area of allotments with extremely healthy looking plants on them – and no wonder! Alongside the road ran an open concrete sewer which ran into cesspits every 100 yards or so, and the gardeners brought their pails to the these pits and having moved the solids away from the top, took this liquid to their patches for irrigation and fertilizer. We were warned in the Lonely Planet Guide not to eat raw salad in restaurants as the Chinese are not too fussy how they wash it – if at all. Now we know why!

There were several occasions when students approached us and wanted to have their photo taken with Edward, and also to talk. Students of English only have each other to talk to most of the time, and they seek out native English speakers in order to practise, and we found it most interesting. We were not able to discuss the political situation, nor did we try to, and we spent some time talking to a young man in Guilin about his job prospects when he finally qualified. He wanted to be a teacher or a guide and if he got a job in the city, his salary of 75 pounds per month would be double what he would be paid if he was sent to the countryside, and where he went was not entirely in his hands. He was not quite clear how he became a guide, but he thought it led to a better standard of living – perhaps he was expecting to get lucrative tips from his European clients.

Daily life goes on, and a feature of Chinese life is early morning exercises, and people partake in these at whatever level they want. Wherever we went, before breakfast they were out in large and small groups practising Tai Chi with a leader, limbering up physically and mentally for the day ahead. Some groups were being quite vigorous and throwing themselves with abandon into their exertions, while others were being much more graceful, holding poses for a few moments before moving to the next one. In contrast there were a few scattered groups of two or three women who were chatting away to each other while moving about in a seemingly unstructured manner.

We saw from our mini-bus later in the day what looked like a labour market place. Groups of men mingled around carrying paintbrushes, hammers and saws, spanners, pitchforks and other equipment, and I was only able to assume that they were advertising their trade, and were for hire. And this was nearly the twenty-first century, not eighteenth century England!

On our arrival at the airport in Beijing, we only had US dollars which we had brought in with us as the only universal money to exchange, so two of us went off following the money exchange signs. We arrived at a dead end and came across an old lady who looked like a lavatory attendant. I waved a bundle of dollars to show what I was looking for, and she said 'Here,' in English, and fished a large roll of Yuan notes out of her apron pocket! She gave us eight Yuan to the dollar, which we thought a bit low, but we needed something to start us off. We went back to the others wondering why it never occurred to us to change our money with a lavatory attendant in the first place! Subsequently we got 8.07 Yuan from a bank where the procedures were very time consuming, and later in a café near The Great Wall, we got 8.20 Yuan, where they were not.

The main roads in Beijing were thoughtfully landscaped, but we wondered at what cost to existing roads and the people who lived in them. Wide dual carriageways with extra lanes for cyclists lined with trees and flowers made for a peaceful atmosphere. With large well-proportioned modern buildings made of glass and concrete, the impression is of a vibrant economy, but one is not too sure of this. It was free and easy to walk down the streets, and crossing the roads was not a problem because there was a footbridge or underpass not far away in any direction. We walked past some street vendors who had spread their goods on cloths on the pavement, and before we could peruse their wares, they all suddenly gathered up their stuff and legged it round the corner. The next thing we saw was a slow-moving police vehicle, and that a 'lookout' must have warned the vendors of their arrival. Obviously then street trading is illegal, or you must have a licence to do it. Elsewhere, just outside the Forbidden City, we fought our way through the very persistent 'gift tat' sellers who accosted us shamelessly on the pavement. Fortunately Bridget had mastered the Chinese for 'not today thank you' or some such phrase, and we got away to a curio market with stalls erected in park-like surroundings. In our own time, we wandered up and down and did one or two deals for paintings on silk, an abacus and an ivory walking stick, and I also bought a copy of Mao's 'Little Red Book' in English, which I may read sometime!

The hotel we stayed in was only 20 minutes walk from Tiananmen Square. It is enormous, the largest square in the world, and is about 100 acres and mostly uncluttered with street furniture. There is a large democratic monument in the middle with inspiring bas-relief sculptures round the base showing how the heroic people overcame tyranny. At the south end two more large sculptures guard the entrance to Mao's tomb, but we did not fancy joining the queues to go inside. At the north end, the Chinese flag is raised at dawn and lowered at dusk everyday, and is guarded by very smart soldiers. Funnily enough, all the soldiers we saw on duty looked very smart, but off duty they looked like scarecrows with their leisure uniforms seeming to be far too large for them. Sitting in the square people-watching, one cannot help thinking of the lone student holding up a tank which had been sent in to break up a protest. That image which had world-wide coverage on TV remains, but the protest was eventually broken up with gunfire leaving many dead and vans carrying protesters away.

Nothing short of a successful revolution will get rid of today's leaders who have such a tight grip on all aspects of daily life. Being a member of 'The Party' is so important in what sort of job you can get, and where you live. Any deviation from the party line – whether actual or imagined – can get you thrown out so that you can only get menial jobs and maybe even sent away from home. Scary, and you can see from the events in Tiananmen Square in 1989 just how far the authorities are prepared to go when they feel that their leadership is being questioned.

Nonetheless the Square is a very impressive place surrounded by State buildings, and at the north end is The Forbidden City, so called because it was the home of the Emperor, his family and court, and no one below a certain rank was allowed inside. The extravagant opulence which surrounded the Emperor is hard to imagine, but in a place such as this some sort of understanding can be made. The area is surrounded by high red-painted walls and encloses about 170 acres, and those who lived there never left it unless they absolutely had to, and this was the case for 500 years through two dynasties. No expense seems to have been spared in the provision of architectural wonders and their decoration. When we at last found the entrance, we hired a tape (spoken by Roger Moore) to help us through the complex which took us round various temples, audience chambers and other buildings dedicated as the 'Hall of Supreme Harmony' or 'Palace of Heavenly Purity' and the like. This is the most complete part of old China left untouched by the communists, and is now officially designated as a museum.

The Emperor was not only the Son of God, but Head of the entire known world, and was revered by his subjects in a manner difficult to visualize. He repaid this reverence with such brutality, having total power over life and death – which was maybe one of the reasons why he was revered so. In each of the throne rooms we saw a gold ball suspended over the throne, and it was said that it would fall on the head of the Emperor if ever he made a false judgement or a decision that would be detrimental to the country. The sexual 'goings-on' in the Palace were as important and as frequent as the political ones. Having a nucleus of people, all with immense power cooped up in this small area, was a perfect atmosphere for intrigue. We had a tiring day of walking in hot autumn sunshine, and at the end of our journey in the Forbidden Palace we followed signs to refreshments, and found ourselves in a delightful courtyard shaded by trees, with the sound of water running over rocks. All this, and the best cup of coffee I had in China set us back a mere one pound each.

The Summer Palace, about an hour from the centre of Beijing, was built as a retreat from the heat of the city. It is now a public park with shady walks and a large lake and many lily ponds set in peaceful galleries. Built 200 years ago, mainly of wood it has been burnt down a number of times – once by the British and French during the opium wars. As with other buildings in China, including the Forbidden City, they were always re-built at once in exactly the same way as they were before. It was a Sunday, and was full of people relaxing as with any city park at a weekend in good weather. Here we saw an old man practising the art of calligraphy. He was using a brush about five feet long, and drawing the characters on paving stones with water. The image stayed for about five minutes before it faded in the hot sun, and was quite fascinating to watch – in fact I found it beautiful to watch anyone writing, including shop girls writing receipts.

Away from the well-landscaped main roads in the city, it was not too difficult to find a bit more squalor. In the side streets there are street traders who are legitimate – well I suppose so because their pitches have a permanency about them – selling all sorts of goods: the mundane for locals mixed with souvenirs for tourists. Off these side streets are hutongs, or alleyways no more than three feet wide, which lead to one or two-room hovels. There are always plenty of public WCs in these areas, because these hovels have no such places, and they contain public washing as well as toilet facilities in them. They are just about OK for the desperate tourist, but they are of the squat variety, and smell rather obnoxious, and one wonders how these Dickensian conditions are allowed to remain – it could be London in the mid nineteenth century.

The outstanding sight in the north is without doubt The Great Wall. Miles and miles of stone walling about 10 to 15 feet wide most of the way, with watchtowers at irregular intervals, is perched on the apex of hills along its length. It was started over 2,000 years ago and work continued on and off until the fifteenth century, and many parts are crumbling and unsafe. Large sections have been repaired, and we went to Jinshanling where we were to start our 10 km walk to Sumatai which was about a mile from the car park to the Wall. It was all uphill, arriving at the first watchtower up a flight of steps with risers varying between three and fifteen inches, and I found all this a bit too much so as I knew that I would hold the others up if I continued, I retreated back to the mini-bus and met the others at Sumatai.

I watched the others go off on the first leg of the Wall, and they reported later that parts were really tough, including one section of a 70 degree slope, and it took them over four hours, much of it over loose stones. As we approached the Wall, a guide attached herself to each of us, and though we tried to shrug them off, they would not go away. I don't know whether we were officially required to employ them, but I really appreciated mine in the way that she held my arm on the way down, and the others were extremely glad of their assistance when the route was unclear. They all carried glossy guide books and trinkets for sale which I refused, and I had the greatest difficulty in getting my guide to accept even a ten Yuan note, but I did eventually persuade her by making her take it on behalf of the child she was obviously carrying. The extraordinary thing was that the guides who had completed a four hour walk, turned round and walked straight back to Jinshanling. The views from the Wall are quite spectacular, as one would expect, and I spent some time gazing over the countryside trying to imagine the Mongol hordes in their efforts to invade their neighbours. The Wall was built to keep them out (it didn't) and the logistics of getting the materials and men to build it would seem overwhelming – on a par with building the pyramids, I suppose.

We flew from Beijing to Xi'an, and found that our accommodation had been upgraded to an en-suite apartment with two bedrooms and a sitting room, which was very acceptable for a couple of nights, and Edward was able to have his own room for a change. Near here is the site of the Army of Terracotta Warriors. In 1976 a peasant who was drilling for some water, uncovered some ancient artifacts, and he reported his find to the authorities. They dug around looking for more and stumbled across this amazing army underground, and are still digging, and at the time we were there, there were 6,000 separate soldiers to be seen. Nothing quite prepares you for the first sight of these life size statues made of terracotta all lined up in battle order. All their faces are different, and it is thought that the stonemasons and sculptors who made them used each other for models. The whole area is covered by a clear span roof, which itself is quite dramatic, and work just keeps on going on further and further into the hillside.

These warriors were made by the Emperor Qin Shi Huang for his own burial chamber some 2,000 years ago, and the countless workers were all executed on the site when it was finished. They were told of a special bonus at the end of the job, and everlasting life in the company of their Emperor was that bonus! There were no written records, and so no one knew of its existence, and it was a good job that the find was made after the cultural revolution of the 1960s was over, otherwise no doubt the Red Guards would have smashed the place to smithereens.

From Xi'an we went to Guilin, an area well known for its limestone karst scenery, and we were able to view this remarkable landscape from a boat sailing down the River Li to Yangshuo for about five hours – and not a minute too long either. Seen from the boat, these phallic hills piercing the valley floor were forever changing their relationship with one another as we drifted downstream, and the fascination with them was endless. We were travelling with David Foster, a geography teacher, and he explained to us exactly how the karsts were formed, which is most interesting, however there is a fanciful tale told that these hills were being driven by a bad king to fill up the sea in order to make his enemy, the sea king, impotent. An ally of the sea king, though, crept into the camp of the bad king one night and stole the magic whip which he was using, so that he had to abandon his project in Guilin. David thought that this was a much better story than his, and said he would use it in his next lesson!

We stopped en route to Yangshuo so that a number of passengers could visit some caves. This one-hour scheduled stop turned out to be over two hours, and while I was sitting on the bank in the sunshine, the boat slipped its moorings and went off downstream without me. It stopped at the point where the cave visitors would emerge, and so I set off on the towpath to rejoin my party, and just before I got there I was stopped by a stream which was too wide to jump. Confronted with the prospect of retracing my steps and taking an alternative path, a ferryman hove into view with a bamboo boat fitted out with four armchairs. He offered to take me across for ten Yuan, but I said I would only pay five Yuan which he accepted, though I would have happily given him 20 Yuan rather than go back!

I watched Chinese peasants at work during this stop, in their fields close by the moorings. These fields were tiny, not much bigger than allotments, and the main crop was rice, with some green vegetables and bamboo growing alongside. Having cut the rice and laid it out on the ground to dry, the peasants were passing sheaves through a foot operated threshing machine no larger than an upright piano. The straw was neatly stacked and thatched in readiness for animal bedding or food in the winter, or even human bedding, I suppose. We saw plenty of water buffalo, goats, ducks and chicken, but no sheep, pigs or cows though there is plenty of pork in Chinese cooking and milk must come from cows.

Only about one fifth of the third largest country in the world can be used for agriculture, and if this is not used efficiently, then the result is famine. This is what happened in the late '50s and early '60s, brought on by the cultural revolution which was an invention of Mao's in order to boost his flagging popularity. This got completely out of hand, and the country is only just getting over it at the turn of the century, some 30 to 40 years later.

The food we enjoyed in China was really tasty. The sweet and sour, crispy dishes and soups, although my experience is not great, were absolutely nothing like you get in an average UK takeaway. The textures and flavours are marvellous, though on the whole breakfasts were not so attractive, which we found out in Beijing where it was not included in the room price. There was a café next door, and we moved in as a group to the mild astonishment of the locals, where we had a bowl of what seemed like partly cooked ravioli-like parcels floating in some rather greasy water. The difficulty of picking these up with chopsticks was only marginally greater than swallowing them! We went to McDonalds the next day which wasn't a great deal better, but at least I got a decent cup of coffee. After this, breakfast was included with the room price. But the memory of Peking duck, and potato and egg soup with sweet corn will linger.

Our surprisingly naïve view of the classless society of the People's Republic of China was rudely shattered at Xi'an airport while we were waiting to board our plane for Guilin. First-class passengers were invited to board before others, which they did except for one. Nobody realised what the holdup was, but we ordinary folk were not allowed on the plane until this passenger turned up. He was roundly booed by those of us waiting, but he just put up two fingers to us – perhaps he was a high ranking official, who knows? The logic of waiting rather than reserving his seat and letting us on board escaped us, but we were in no great hurry, and had one of the best on-board meals ever, with fresh rice and pork. Apart from this incident we were very well looked after and the airports and the systems were pretty efficient. They could learn a little courtesy though, and this seemed to apply to whatever we did or wherever we went.

We went to China with Caroline and Mike Elmett, and Sue and David Foster. Caroline has had experience of travelling, and was most efficient in arranging all our flights, hotels and programme, and I went with her to the Chinese Embassy to get visas for our trip. We had all seven passports with us, and there seemed to be a lot of people there, and we were despondent at getting through in less than four hours or so. We were given seven forms to fill in on which signatures were required, so I immediately thought that we would have to go home to get them. 'Oh, no,' said Caroline, who explained that she had signed other people's forms loads of times, and she wasn't going to stop now! So this is what we did. I copied Bridget's and Edward's signatures, while Caroline not only signed for her husband, but for the Fosters as well. At least I only did it for my family.

We took a ticket, and sat in what was supposed to be an orderly numbered queue, and mainly it was, but odd people walked up to the counter with from time to time without being told to go away. As our number was approaching, we walked up to the window of the counter, and even then we had to elbow away a queue jumper, and we were told to come back and collect our visas in ten days time. This normally takes only five days, but the next week was a long public holiday to celebrate 50 years of the People's Republic of China, and so the embassy was going to be closed so that they could all go home to join in the celebrations. It took us two hours to get the applications in, and half an hour to collect them which Caroline reckoned was some sort of record!

This was a trip that was memorable for many things, but walking on the Great Wall and seeing the Terracotta Warriors were the undoubted highlights.

Floating market, Damnoen Saduak

Salt Flats Samut Phrakan on Route 35

The Great Wall of China

Bangkok Expressways from top of Bayoke Tower

Ankgor Wat, Seam Reap, Cambodia

Long Neck Women, Karen Tribe, N. Thailand

Schwedegon Pagoda, Rangoon, Burma

Fishing on Lake Inle, Burma

Cigar Manufacture, Lake Inle

Elephant stables, Ayutthaya

Star Ferry, Kowloon, Hong Kong

Hanoi Street, Vietnam

Typical street food stall, Bangkok

Ayutthaya

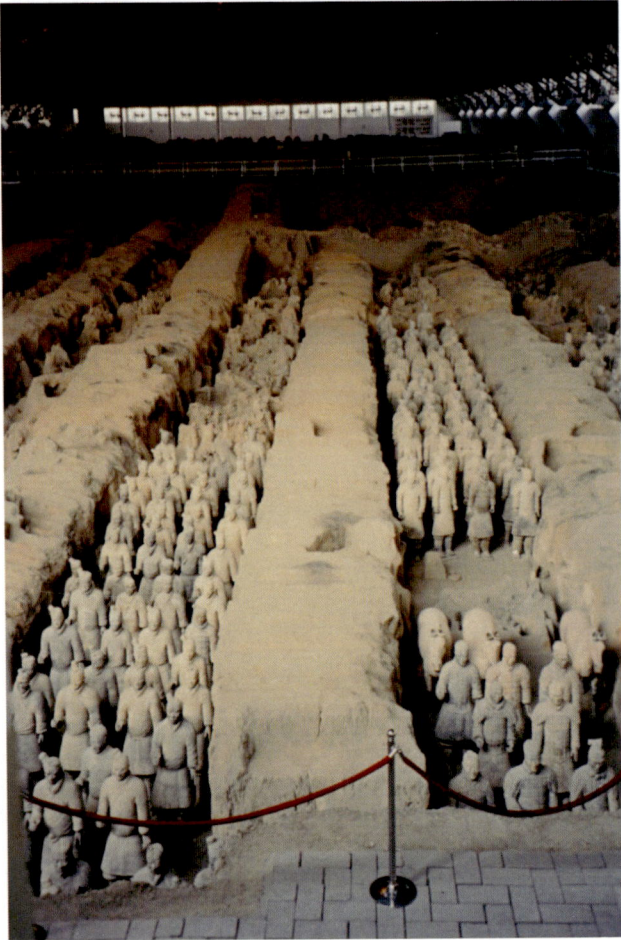

Terra Cotta Warriors, Xian – China

Painting Chinese Characters with water, Beijing

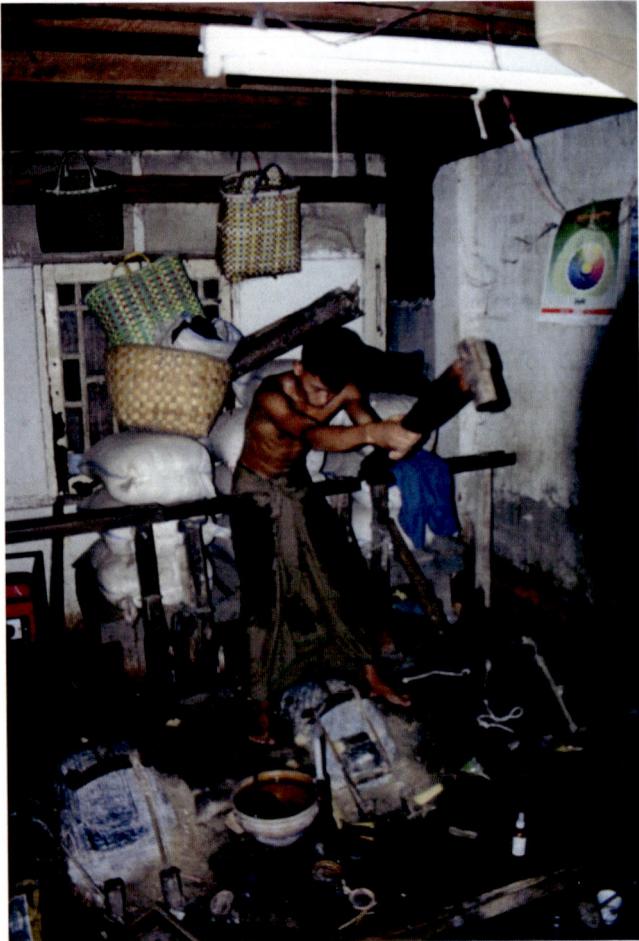

Manufacturing merit-making gold leaf, Burma

CHAPTER 12

Kanchanaburi and Hellfire Pass February 2000

While in Kanchanaburi for the weekend, we visited the two museums there, dedicated to the Second World War in general, and the building of the Death Railway in particular. These museums have been updated and improved a great deal since, but they were both rather shoddy and run in an amateurish way when we first went there. There was a wealth of interesting material on show, poorly presented and much of it with only Thai labelling, but a great deal was very moving, particularly the mock up of a bamboo hut that prisoners of war had to live in. They had a mere two feet of space each on a six-foot bamboo mattress, which ran down the length of the hut like a long shelf, about three feet off the ground.

The Japanese, in order to pursue their aims of driving the British out of Burma and India (having already achieved these aims in Malaya and Singapore), invaded Thailand in 1942. A neutral country, the pragmatic Thais allowed them in after a token resistance. The supply routes from Japan to Burma were too long and dangerous, so the Japanese decided to build a railway link through the mountainous region of West Thailand in the Kanchanaburi region. There were many cuttings to dig, and many bridges to build – the most famous one, of course, being the one over the River Kwai.

Using Allied prisoners of war as labour as well as many Thais and other nationalities, the line was completed in 15 months – all 415 miles of it – at the cost of nearly 100,000 lives. Over 13,000 were prisoners of war, and over 80,000 were Asian labourers. 6,000 Australian and Dutch, as well as British servicemen, are laid out to rest in beautifully kept cemeteries in the town. Walking around I felt a great deal of sadness for the men who had died, and also for their families. I was particularly moved when I came across the grave of a young soldier who had died on my thirteenth birthday in 1942. I don't know why, except that it was a day of happiness for me, but one of misery for his family. I am lucky to have been too young to take part in this conflict.

On an impulse during that weekend we drove 80 km west of the town to visit Hellfire Pass, so named by the prisoners because of the eerie light and shadows thrown up by the bonfires which were the only source of illumination after dark. The project was so far behind schedule that work had to go on round the clock, or the Japanese engineers would have incurred the severe displeasure of their High Command. Further, the treatment of the prisoners was unbelievably cruel. With only one meal of watery rice per day, malnutrition led to serious related diseases and ailments – small scratches would not heal and these led to severe ulcers. Prisoners thought to be slacking were beaten by the guards without mercy – often to death, which in many cases must have been a blessed relief.

Medical treatment was virtually non-existent, but the doctors among the prisoners made their own surgical instruments in order to perform the most rudimentary operations. There was a clandestine network of Thais, who, at great risk of death or worse to themselves, supplied the camps with just a few of the needs of the medics. They were a group of very brave people, whose assistance to the humanitarian war effort cannot be too highly appreciated.

At the site of Hellfire Pass, the Australians have built a superb museum and memorial to the thousands who died during the construction of the railway. Modern, spacious and air-conditioned, it tells the story of the building of the railway in general and this pass in particular, with models, artefacts found in and around the area, an old film and photographs, all with a concise text. Such a contrast to the museums we found in the town when we first went there. They have constructed a walk through the jungle down a steep hill to a viewing area, where you can see the pass from above. About 100 metres long and 20 metres deep, the cutting has sheer walls just wide enough to allow a train to pass through. This solid rock was mainly cut out with chisels and sledgehammers by hand, and carried away in wicker baskets. There is evidence that in order to speed things up in the later stages, the workers were given at least one pneumatic drill, as there is part of a broken bit wedged in the face of the rock.

At ground level the whole thing looks so amazingly unlikely to have been built by hand, and with just a few rails and sleepers left to show where the line was, all I could do was to stand and wonder at the crazy ambitions of military regimes in those not-so-far-off days of the last century. A little way further on, a trestle bridge had been built, mainly of bamboo tied together with pieces of bark. It clung to the side of the cliff in an apparently tenuous manner, although it was newly constructed by the museum staff. The main supports were let into holes made in the rock floor, and a favourite trick of sabotage was to fill the holes with something unstable before putting in the feet of the supports, so that the bridge itself became unstable. On the whole, though, it was an amazing engineering feat by the Japanese engineers to construct this railway where they did, which was strong enough to support the weight of a train.

Work on these sections of the railway would have been marginally less disagreeable than in the cuttings, as at least the workers would catch any breeze going. With humidity at 90 per cent in August and September and with no air flow in the cuttings, it must have been totally debilitating.

The Allies took to bombing the line wherever they could, especially the bridges. The prisoners were taken to the damaged parts and some had to make repairs, while others carried supplies from one train to another across the damaged section. Prisoners were also used as human shields, but this unfortunately did not stop the bombing. Apart from the beatings, the Japanese inflicted awful punishments on their prisoners, for example, having been given a heavy rock, they had to stand still in the hot sun, holding the rock over their heads; or being tied up by their thumbs to a branch of a tree, with only their toes touching the ground – there must be many more not documented.

The railway was built in 1942 and 1943, but it was not until August 1945 that the war in the Far East was over, three months after the war in Europe, and the prisoners had to endure their suffering right up to the end. Many of those who survived came home physically and mentally scarred, unable to take up their lives where they left off.

There are many good and inexpensive restaurants here, and the war and the suffering of those days (on which the busy tourist trade relies) seems a long way off while enjoying a cool beer on a floating restaurant watching the bridge. A twelve-coach train passes over it once a day from Bangkok and goes up the line for about 6 km and then returns. Tourists are crossing the bridge all day long on foot, and they just have to get out of the way when the train goes by. There is no regulation about clearing them before the train can cross, though nobody ever seems to get hurt. I can't see this happening in the UK without whistles and warnings galore where 'Elf & Safety' rules OK!

CHAPTER 13

Angkor Wat and Cambodia, April 2000

Our four-day visit to Cambodia was not all cultural sightseeing, though much of the time was spent in and around the old temples. Angkor is an ancient city, which was the capital of the Khmer Empire from about 8OO to 1400 AD. It covers a large area in which each successive king thought it necessary to build more temples, of which the best known, largest and in the best state of repair, is Angkor Wat.

The Empire stretched from Vietnam to Laos through Northern Thailand to the borders of Burma. In the late fourteenth century and early fifteenth it was disintegrating, and the people moved their capital to Phnom Penh in order to escape the attentions of their marauding neighbours. Angkor thus became less and less used as the amenities broke down through lack of maintenance, and eventually became deserted. Monks used to go back from time to time, but even this stopped after a while. It was always known that there was a city here, and it gradually became overgrown by the jungle. In the middle of the nineteenth century, some French archaeologists (Cambodia was a French colony at the time) went looking for it, and over the next 60 years cleared the jungle from the sites and started reconstruction work.

One of the reasons that the buildings fell into disrepair was that all the roofs were corbelled, and arches were not held in place with a key-stone. This method of construction had not been stumbled upon, which had been known in Europe, but was not known in Central and South America either during the same period. Trees and plants grew through the masonry, thus destroying the structure and fabric of the stonework. Plants grow so quickly in the tropics that this process did not take very long. Now trees and walls exist in a symbiotic relationship.

What the French explorers found was breathtaking. Every wall in Angkor is covered in bas-relief work depicting stories largely from India from the Ramayana, of the gods Shiva and Vishnu. And what walls are not telling these stories are covered with floral patterns or images of gods and kings. Indian influence is very strong here, as Cambodia lies on the trading route between India and China. The intricacy of the work is amazing, and there are several kilometres of walls in all. The detail in one area was so fine and detailed, and the guide book explained that when an extension had been built, this section had been covered up with earth, so that it had been protected from the weather. It had been carefully excavated, and was now in a deep trench. This was at Angkor Thom.

We had a guide and a car plus driver for four days, and we saw many of the ancient sites, including Tha Phrom, which is largely un-restored and has jungle growing in it. The roots of banyan trees are spreading round the walls in a love-hate relationship, on the one hand destroying the fabric and on the other hand preventing them from falling down. Masonry is left where it fell, and although areas are cordoned off, one is not quite sure when the next bit is going to fall off!

One of the more remarkable things about the whole area is that the temples and king's palaces (often the same place) were the only buildings made of stone. The inhabitants, and at its peak it is said that there were about one million of them, lived in bamboo and rush houses which have long since disappeared. So unlike the great buildings of Europe, like Rouen Cathedral and St. Paul's which were built at about the same time, where street clutter such as traffic lights, video shops and McDonalds hinder the view, these temples can be seen in their full glory from almost any angle.

Later on in the day we climbed a steep hill to a ruined temple, Phnom Bakeng, not by a path or steps, but a wide track made up of rocks and loose stones. For me it was definitely a hands-and-feet climb, and it took nearly half an hour, with breathing stops for all of us. The temple at the top was not the point of the climb, really, but the view. To the west, the sun was setting over distant hills, with its reflection in water surrounded by trees. To the east, the five stupas of Angkor Wat can be seen blood red in the setting sun. But not today: at the crucial moment the sun went behind a layer of cloud, and we were denied this spectacle at the last minute. And suddenly it was dark as tends to happen in the tropics. We went down by a longer but safer route by way of a hairpin path – I didn't fancy the hill, with its loose surface, going down in the dark.

The steps of the temples that we had to climb up and down were nearly as bad as those on the Great Wall in China, which we had visited last year. With 6" treads and up to 15" risers not only was it difficult placing my feet on the steps, but each one was a tough climb as well. For me it was hands and feet all the way up, and it was worse coming down. I took one sideways step at a time always holding onto something, and it was quite fearsome looking down – I can't think why we do it! But we made the effort, and it was always worthwhile.

Rather too many Wats on our first day and a half, we were taken on a 30 km drive to the South to a fishing village. The drive through the suburbs of Siem Reap (where we were staying) took us along roads lined with the poorest of bamboo and rush dwellings, with one or two rooms, on stilts on the river bank. The people were just sitting around and their naked children (many of whom were for sale, our guide told us) were playing in the dust or the murky-looking river. Pol Pot's communist experiment of the late 1970s managed to decimate ruthlessly not only the population, but the economy as well. All is still a long way from recovery. The corruption-infested politics and politicians have done little or nothing for the poor at the bottom of the heap, most of whom have nowhere to go. I suppose selling your children for whatever purpose, be it for prostitution or for adoption by a European family, is an attractive prospect. After all, they are a renewable resource, aren't they?

The tarmac road ran out into a dirt track full of pot-holes and raised like a causeway over flat rice fields on both sides. After half an hour of this, the road ended in the poorest of poor looking villages, absolutely stinking of fish meal. In the nearby river sat about ten to twenty boats with canopies over them, and with comfortable wicker chairs on board, waiting to take tourists to the fishing village on the lake. Being the end of the dry season, the water was at its lowest, and our boatman had to wade out into the river to get the boat and having done so, we had to walk along a flimsy bouncing plank to get aboard. This accomplished, we were glad to be off that terrible road, and the boatman still had to push the boat until it was deep enough to start the engine.

Eventually we were on our way, and the river twisted and turned, and we were looking up into impenetrable jungle on both sides and it was easy to imagine that we were intrepid Victorian explorers navigating unknown waters for the first time. This fantasy diminished somewhat each time we met a boatload of tourists coming the other way! The river opened up on to a wide plain and then flowed into an inland sea called Le Grand Lac. Pretty sizeable now, it doubles in size during the wet season because the river that drains it into the Mekong River in the dry season reverses its flow when the Mekong floods in the rainy season, and fills it up again.

House boats were dotted about near the shore whichever way you looked, mainly occupied by fishermen and their families. We chugged through this village to a fish farm where there was a small area of lake of about thirty by thirty feet netted to keep fish in and predators out. The house boat here was smaller than the fish pen, with two rooms and a landing stage. A family lived here with two monkeys, a python, a sloth, some fancy tropical fish and some pelicans. They sold cold drinks and souvenirs to tourists, and they probably made a better living doing that than fishing. The family appeared to be very happy, but I suppose they would be with some unimaginably wealthy tourists on board. On our way back as dusk approached, there seemed to be no definition between sea and sky in the setting sun, and we enjoyed the surreal but fleeting impression of fishing boats seemingly floating in space.

The next day we took another long drive into the country to a little visited temple called Banteay Srei. Dedicated to the god Shiva and only partially restored, the floral carving in the pink sandstone is truly exquisite and memorable. In this area the inhabitants seemed to be a little better off than those we visited yesterday, and they had little gardens around their houses, enclosed with a fence.

On the way back to our hotel, we visited a landmine museum which is the home of a young man who fought for the Khmer Rouge when aged 14, was captured, and fought for the Royal Forces. He has filled his small garden with defused mines, just to show how easy it was to plant them, and how difficult to it was to find them. There are piles of old mines to look at of all different types as well as all sorts of decaying and old ordnance from the past war. There were personal stories and paintings to illustrate different events of this man's short life, and once again I felt glad that I have never been involved in any military conflict.

Later we visited the memorial to the Killing Fields of Siem Reap. Not as large by a long way as that outside Phnom Penh, where 20,000 people were bludgeoned to death (to save bullets), but gruesome enough. Human skulls and bones are exhibited in a glass-sided case for all to see, and when there is enough money they will be given a decent burial.

The sights and sounds of a city leave memories: the squealing of pigs on their way to slaughter – not in a lorry or pickup, but upside down in a cradle on the back of a motor bike, with their legs in the air. Not to be forgotten. Another sight was that of hundreds of men and women dredging the moat round Angkor Wat by hand. The water being at its lowest just now, it was no more than waist high, and they were dragging weeds to the water's edge where they were being collected by lorry. It is a good job in this hot weather with high humidity - not that we wanted to do it even though we did get very hot and wet tramping around the temples.

One of the reasons for the great success of the Khmers, who acquired and maintained an empire for 500 to 600 years, was the way in which they managed their water. Great reservoirs were constructed, usually with a small island in the middle with a temple on it. These reservoirs silted up over the years, but there was always another one ready to take over the important job of irrigating the rice paddies, and the water was directed along channels in a very sophisticated manner. It does seem obvious in hindsight, but one of the reasons for the decline of the empire was the neglect by later kings of the principles of hydraulics practised by earlier rulers. Some recent research suggests that Angkor's success was partly to blame for the silting up of the reservoirs and canals, as the existing infrastructure was unable to cope with the increasing population. To feed all these people, more trees had to be cut down on the hillsides to grow more rice, which in turn led to more run-off when it rained, thus leading to more silting up, which in its turn made less water available for irrigation.

An excellent, but short visit, and now we would like to see more of Cambodia and go to Phnom Penh.

CHAPTER 14

North Thailand, April 2000

We visited North Thailand during the same Easter holidays after we had returned from Cambodia. It is quite different from the Central Plain area of Bangkok, which is totally flat (as, of course, plains tend to be!) and is hilly without being mountainous. There are stunning views of tree-covered hills, and rivers that carve their way through the countryside in their alternate mad rush to the sea and placid calm. These steep-sided hills swoop down into narrow valleys and whoosh up again forming a V, with a narrow band of very fertile soil on each side of a river at the bottom. Other hills open up on to a wider valley before reaching for the skies again. Rice is virtually the only (legal) crop here, and they get at least two crops per year.

We flew to Chiang Mai and then to Mae Hong Son in the west of the region; a delightful little town, with its airport not far from the main street. We booked a car and driver for the next day as soon as we got to the hotel, and went on an all-day excursion round the area. We started in the market place. Thailand seems to be a country of street markets, and as one of the national pastimes is shopping, they fill a need. The fresh produce in this one, though, looked as fresh as if it had been harvested only minutes earlier, and the meats looked as if they were still warm (though I am not sure how I would think of this later in the day after they had been out in the hot sun for a

99

while). As usual, almost anything you could possibly want was on sale – and very cheap by UK standards.

From there we boarded a narrow boat for a trip down the River Pi. For nearly an hour I sat on a rush mat as there were no seats on this boat, but the scenery we passed through had my attention to such an extent that I gave no thought to my discomfort. Steep-sided gorges gave way to tree-covered hills and then an open plain to our destination. On the way we negotiated rapids, not exactly what you would call white water, but very gentle ones where the flow of water was just a little quicker over the shallow floor.

Along the banks, we passed women washing their clothes in the river, men fishing both with rod and line and with nets, and children swimming. Some of them waved and allowed us to take photographs, but others turned their backs on us. Muslims as well as Buddhists believe that having their photo taken removes part of their soul, and although 90 per cent of the population of Thailand is Buddhist, there are a significant number of Muslims and a few Christians. At one point, the boat shuddered to a stop and so did the engine. Before I had time to register this event as a calamity, the boatman jumped out and gave the boat a push off the bottom of the river! As we had stopped, he thought he might as well fill the reservoir of the water-cooled engine, then we were on our way again.

We landed on the shore under a road bridge, and as I climbed unsteadily out of it along a wobbly plank, I could see no signs of life anywhere, only jungle. Were we being kidnapped? These things do happen, it's not unknown. But no, as we climbed the bank to the road, our car and guide were waiting for us, and we were taken to a hill-tribe village. There are six main peoples who live in the hills, whose ancestors had escaped from persecution in their own countries such as China and Burma, and set up their own communities in Thailand.

Their life depended on subsistence agriculture, and they used the 'slash and burn' technique, which is still used to a lesser extent, as it is very harmful to the environment. We saw many steep and bare hillsides prepared in this manner over the years, and we cannot imagine how they keep the soil from washing away during the rainy season. The answer is that they probably don't. Rice is not grown on the hillsides, as that crop needs level ground, and unless they grow poppies, we were not sure what it was used for. Opium poppy growing became a very useful cash crop for these people to satisfy the need of the whole of South and East Asia. Illegal of course, and the government is fighting an uphill battle to stop it, but some areas are so remote, it is very difficult. What makes it even more difficult is that many of those in authority are making a decent living in turning a blind eye to what goes on (so I am given to understand). One way of combating the problem is to make the villages more accessible and encourage tourism. So many of them now have good roads to them and through them, replacing the dirt tracks of a few years ago.

The first village we went to was peopled by the Karen tribe, who came from Burma. The home of the so-called 'Long Neck' women who I remember reading about in the National Geographic magazine when I was a boy before the war, never dreaming for an instant that one day I would meet and speak with them. From the age of three or four, brass rings are fitted round their necks, adding to them over the years until they have 10 or 12. It was originally done as a protection from wild animals, then as a beauty treatment and now as a tourist attraction. This is really sad, as it is horribly disfiguring for the poor girls, though it is only those who are born on a Wednesday who have this honour bestowed on them, yet it doesn't even lengthen their necks. It is the weight of the rings pushing down and crushing the rib cage that makes the neck look long, and at the throat the rings make it difficult for them to speak properly. The girls can opt out, but if they do not do so by their mid-teens at the latest, their neck muscles atrophy, and they would never be able to hold their heads up again unaided.

This village is called Noi Soi, and alongside the 'long-necks' live the 'long-eared' women. These people insert a ring or disc of perhaps 1" to 2" in diameter in their earlobes so that the ears hang down to double their natural size. They also wrap brass rings round their legs and ankles making for more disfigurement. It seems to be a bit like the binding of the feet of young Chinese girls, but not so cruel. They make a living by charging a small fee for photographs, and selling their home-made artefacts. The 'long-necks' are Buddhist, and the 'long-ears' are Catholic, so we were told, and they live in harmony with each other. They fled from Burma in the 1980s. All the different tribes wear distinctive clothing and headgear, brightly coloured with reds, blues and white on basically black garments, in which they look very ethnic. Many of them brighten up the streets of Bangkok where they sell bangles and trinkets, mainly to willing tourists.

From here we drove down the road for a few kilometres, to find two elephants waiting for us – one a large male and the other a smaller female. I took the female by myself, while Bridget and Edward took the male, which was probably four or five feet taller. We spent an hour on the backs of these magnificent animals, moving at a seemingly leisurely pace through the jungle tracks, finishing up by fording the river where it was about five feet deep with the water well up the side of the beast. Fortunately, neither of our mounts wanted a shower while we were on board, but in the heat it would not have been totally unwelcome! This is an experience I would gladly repeat, if only to give employment to the elephants and their mahouts. They are becoming rather a nuisance in Bangkok where they roam about, with their keepers offering food for tourists to buy and feed them. We do this when we can as they are such lovely animals, and with the restrictions on logging, which was their main employment, they have little to do in the jungle but still need to eat masses of food. A golfing friend put himself out of action for six months by putting a small bunch of bananas straight into an elephant's mouth, and suffered a nasty injury to his hand. He now knows that you should only offer food by way if its trunk!

On a visit to an ornamental park, we were taken to see some gigantic catfish and carp in an underground pool. There is some religious significance to these fish and where they live, and Buddhists 'make merit' by feeding them. So do tourists, and food is on sale nearby (you are not allowed to feed them with anything else), so it is no wonder that the fish are so enormous with all that food. All sorts of trees are in the park, mainly teak, bamboo and tongtun. This last is a very slender and fast-growing tree with very large leaves of about 18" by 12" which are dried and used as shingles on the roofs of houses, and are also used for wrapping up food for cooking on open fires. On the way out we saw a chameleon clinging to the side of a tree – a great photo opportunity – but I wondered later whether it was made of plastic! I'll never know.

There were some hot springs in this park, and though the water was very hot there were no geysers or any indication where the water came from. There was a woman giving facial treatments with the mud that came up with the water, and Bridget allowed herself to be treated. Edward and I meanwhile enjoyed watching this performance, and seeing Bridget trying not to laugh while the mud was drying on her face. We did not laugh a little later on as we encountered a vendor selling honey-comb. The guide bought a piece for himself and offered some to us. It was of irregular shape and must have come from the wild, and I refused because it was too sickly and sweet, but Bridget accepted so as not to hurt the guide's feelings.So he broke off a bite-sized piece, and in it she saw the grubs of the bees in the comb, but to her credit she forced it down with a smile, though I must say that I was glad that I had refused the offer earlier.

Until now it had been a remarkably Wat-free day, but we did have to go up a steep hill overlooking Mae Hong Son to see a magnificent temple, with beautifully proportioned stupas (steeples). The view over the town was splendid and it was also overlooking the airport where it was quite strange to see planes landing and taking off below us. Finally at the end of a busy day we went to have a really delicious meal at Lucky's Bar, which is where we fell into conversation the previous night with our guide of today. Just as we were going to leave, the heavens opened with the mother and father of an electric storm, so we had to stay for some more drinks. Too bad! There were not many tourists about, and we were made very welcome.

We visited more hill tribes the next day, and found some far more friendly than others. The Hmong and Thai Yai people were very persistent in trying to sell us something, and seem to be unable to speak anything coherently as far as I could make out which became irritating after a bit. They must have developed very thick skins since becoming tourist attractions. The friendliest were the Chinese from what is known as the KMT village. When Mao finally established communism in China in 1949, the main body of Chiang Kai Chek's army – the Kumintang – withdrew to Formosa (now Taiwan), and small parties escaped into Burma and Thailand with the idea that they could perhaps form a pincer movement and overthrow Mao in the course of time. Some hopes! In this village people came up and talked to us; one of them spoke English reasonably well, having learnt it in Burma, but an old soldier came up and he couldn't speak a word of it. Actually this old man became my best friend for the day after I had given him a cigar which had only cost me 1p, and as well as not being able to speak English he was unable to make himself understood even by sign language. I did not know whether he was under the influence of booze, opium or any other drug for that matter – or maybe he was just a little simple. Anyway he befriended me, and insisted that we all took photographs of him with us; it would have been nice to have had a Polaroid.

Most of the dwellings, and I hesitate to call them houses as many of them were what we would call a garden shed in need of repair, had makeshift fences round them with sows and piglets, chicken and chicks, dogs and puppies, cats and kittens and ducks and ducklings all apparently living in harmony with one another. Of course they all escaped from their own allotments, and wandered all over the village, but I suppose they got back to the right place when they needed to. Some houses, especially in the KMT villages, are built more substantially with dried mud blocks plastered over, and with corrugated iron roofs rather than tongtun leaves. Some of these were shops, and we bought some green tea which had been drying in the sun, and some cigars, which is why I was able to give some to my new best friend. Wherever we went we were welcomed with smiles and a cup of green tea, and we came away with a warm feeling.

Thailand was celebrating Songkran that week. This is the four day festival which marks not only the old New Year, but the end of the dry season. The custom is to throw water at anybody and everybody during the whole of this period, and it makes no difference who you are. Tourists are particularly popular targets, and we got more than our share of a dousing in the back of a pick-up in which we had unwisely rolled up the side curtains. The driver seemed to take great pleasure in slowing down when he saw a gang of youths, and indicated that he had some tourists on board. Bridget was particularly unlucky in getting the whole of a bucket of water over her, and she stayed cold until we stopped and she was able get out into the sun. It really is a most tiresome custom, but I had to put a smile on my face so as not to be called a miserable old git!

Chiang Rai was the next centre we visited and we struck a real bull's eye with the accommodation that we had selected from The Lonely Planet Guide. We had phoned up for a room for three, and having booked it we felt good – until we arrived. It turned out to be a real back-packer's hostel, and was full of people with long uncombed (and apparently unwashed) hair and trekking boots. We were given a chalet with three beds and a shower in one corner, and also a lavatory, so it could be called en suite I suppose! As it was full of mosquitoes, the first thing we did was to buy a tin of repellent at a nearby shop. We were not quite sure how clean the blankets were, but we had a sheet each which looked OK.

We had a very basic meal in the open-air restaurant, and went to bed early feeling very privileged to have experienced at first hand how the other half live. We had booked for three nights, but decided not to look for anywhere else because we didn't want to spend time away from our projected days out. This time we went in a mini-bus, which was insulated from the water throwers, and visited more hill tribe villages. This may sound as though we were doing the same thing each day, but each tribe is very different to another. The first one we went to was the Mien Tribe, and we were taken into their houses to see how they lived, and three rooms seemed to be enough for 8, 10 or even 12 people – it wasn't quite clear how many souls occupied this bungalow. There was a dirt floor, and a common room of about 20ft by 20ft in the middle, which housed a colour TV and little else. At each end there was a bedroom, each half that size, with hammocks hanging from all points. There was no sign of any sanitary arrangements, so I suppose the jungle sufficed.

Next we went to a village of the Akha Tribe, and it could not have been more different. We had to climb up steps to the living area, as the houses were built on stilts either to keep them free from flooding or as protection from wild animals. These were much the same size as the last ones, but the floor was made of woven split bamboo, and seemed vary unstable. The walls were the same, and tongtun leaves were laid on the bamboo on the roof to keep the rain out. In the middle of this, the occupant was cooking on an open fire! The fire was on an iron base and the smoke was going out through a hole in the roof, but not before it blackened the ceiling. It looked highly dangerous, and the fire risk overwhelming, but I suppose they knew what they were doing.

Mae Sai is a town on the border with Burma, and this border is the River Ruak, a tributary of the Mekong, which runs between that town and Tachilek, its sister town in Burma. By paying the Burmese border guards US$5 each, we got a day visa to cross over, and it was very disappointing. Obviously much poorer and more run down than Thailand, the houses and shops looked dirty, and the roads full of pot-holes and in serious need of repair. Songkran was in full swing here as well, and so within half an hour we were back in Thailand, with only a couple of jade bangles to show for our visit. I suppose you can't judge a country by its border towns, after all England is not judged by Dover or France by Calais, so we will go on a proper visit to Burma one day.

The Golden Triangle was in years gone by the centre of the opium trade. Being on the confluence of the rivers Ruak and Mekong it was very close to Burma and Laos and so very convenient for the illegal traffic. We visited a very poorly mounted museum about the opium trade, in which there was a wealth of jumbled up but interesting material, and we got an idea of what went on in the nineteenth century. Opium was transported on the backs of mules along jungle trails at great risk from the law, but at even greater risk from rival gangs of dealers. It is much the same now with heroin on the western borders of Thailand, though not so much here. It is a very difficult trade to control, because it is said that those whose job it is to police it find it very lucrative to turn a blind eye, and of course the rewards are so high.

We couldn't resist the opportunity of taking a trip on the Mekong in a small boat. Even at the end of the dry season, it is still a mighty river, though there were plenty of sand banks showing. When the snows melt in Tibet and the monsoon rains fall, it will rise by 30 feet or more and it becomes a formidable river, but today it was placid and we were taken across to Laos, where we climbed up a steep bank to the customs post. This turned out to be a policeman sitting under an umbrella, who waved us through with a smile in stark contrast to the singularly unfriendly Burmese. The small village was completely given over to the selling of souvenirs, local beer (OK), and postcards ready for posting with a local stamp. Back downstream to meet our guide again, we passed an island in the middle of the river on which they grow potatoes during the dry season, and they were harvesting them. Knowing just when the river is about to flood is the key to good husbandry here.

The Laotians are even poorer than the Cambodians whom we visited earlier, and are almost pathetically grateful for our trade, so we did not attempt to barter as their need was much greater than ours – anyway how much discount can one expect on one pound! Not for the first time did I ponder the question of why communist countries seem to be inhabited by the poorest people – could it be anything to do with the greed of those in power? Burma, which we visited later on, is much the same.

We checked out of the hostel in the morning, and the best bit was the bill of 20 pounds for three people for three nights! We had to spend the day in Chiang Rai, and as it was a holiday, everything was shut except for an indifferent café. It was like a provincial market town on a Sunday in the 1950s – dead. We got to Chiang Mai to find that the hotel that I had booked was full as our e-mail had not arrived. The taxi driver took us around and found a perfectly acceptable one with a swimming pool, and as it was 8.30pm by now, we were just a little concerned. Clean sheets and a soft bed were a great treat after the last three days, and we went to sleep very soundly after a little supper.

Capital of the area before Thailand became unified under one king, the old town is surrounded by a square wall inside a moat, and within, the town is laid out on a grid plan which is quite easy to follow on the map. We looked at some stunning gold decorations in Wat Phra Singh and also some beautiful carved teak in the meeting house attached to the wat. Then a couple of hours in a bar with a pool table in it gave us the opportunity to enjoy a liquid lunch which we slept off by the swimming pool until it was time to go to the Night Bazaar. This is a feature of Chiang Mai, and firmly on the tourist trail, though I am not quite sure why, because it is only a large street market that is not open in the daytime. Things are much cheaper than in the Bangkok markets, so we stocked up on some bargains that were not to be missed.

Again, following the tourist trail we visited the San Kamphaeng Road, where there is a silk factory, a semi-precious gem factory, a woodworking centre, a lacquer factory and an umbrella factory, in fact, an area totally dedicated to tourists. But watching the artisans at work was fascinating – silversmiths working on filigree with tiny fretsaws, the deft hands of the lacquer painters, and the wood carvers with their old handtools which looked as if they had been handed down from generation to generation. These last were sitting on the floor holding the wood between their feet, and this looked highly dangerous! We were invited to have a go at carving a piece of softwood with our names, which we did (but not using our feet as a vice!) and so our visit is recorded for ever.

Finally we took a boat for a relaxing afternoon up the river Ping, stopping at a small garden where the owner had planted all manner of plants found in Thailand. It was a blaze of colour, and though the owner only spoke a little English, Bridget spoke enough Thai for them to understand one another. The garden really was full of very healthy looking plants – they do say that the soil is so fertile in Thailand that if you plant a stone it will grow, but you still have to look after the plants and keep them free of pests, which the owner here was doing in a most loving manner.

CHAPTER 15

Sri Lanka, September 2000

I went off from the airport on a Thursday for a golfing trip with 20 others from the British Club of Bangkok, and we were to be away from Friday until Monday, so I was on my own as Bridget was unable to miss two days of school. We played three rounds of golf, spent four nights in three different hotels, spent six hours in an aeroplane and 20 hours on a bus. We saw quite a bit of the country from sea level to 6,000 feet.

Our first night was in Negumba, about an hour from Colombo airport. It was late, so while several members of the party repaired to the bar I fell into bed exhausted, although I had done little all day. I awoke to find that my room opened onto the beach, and so I took an early morning walk, and looking across the Indian Ocean over the breakers which were pounding the sand, I mused on the fact that the next stop was Somalia. Sailing across my line of view was a flotilla of fishing boats, and with the sun from behind me catching the tops of their sails and rigging, the scene gave me a sensation of age-old timelessness.

During a five-hour journey to Kandy, we passed through the prosperous homes in the suburbs of Negumbo, which increasingly gave way to more humble dwellings and then to the shacks of the really poor in the countryside. Coconut plantations lined the route we took, right up to the road and the scary method of harvesting was there to see: ropes were strung from the tops of these trees about 50 or 60 feet from the ground and used as walkways for the pickers to scramble from tree to tree without having to come down to the ground each time they finished one, throwing the coconuts down to their colleagues below. I don't think my apple pickers would have thought much of this system!

Our first game of golf was in the afternoon at the Victoria Golf Club in Kandy. Quite unlike the manicured courses in Bangkok, the fairways and greens were well looked after, but the rough really was rough and it usually cost a shot to get out of the clinging clover-type grass on the semi-rough, and two shots to get out of the thick rough. My caddy was excellent, and not only gave me good lines on the greens, but after watching me play three or four shots knew exactly what club I needed – and I quickly learnt not to argue! Accompanying our game were two fore-caddies who found and marked our tee shots, several of which I would have given up for lost. This certainly speeds the game up! The high point of my game on this trip was achieved on the short eighth (which was my finishing hole), where I put my ball 12" from the pin, getting a birdie and winning three golf balls. The next day we played a match against the club members, but it was rather spoilt by torrential rain which was followed by on-off rain and drizzle.

Somewhat refreshed by our hosts laying on a delicious barbeque after the match, we set off on a five hour coach ride to Nuwara Eliya. Travelling in daylight for the first two hours of the journey, we passed through jungle scenery and several small towns which were teeming with life. Most of the shop signs were in English, and one could have been forgiven for thinking that you were in the streets of, say, Bradford. Apparently some years ago it was felt politically correct to try and eradicate connections with their colonial past, and English was taken out of the school curriculum, but this proved to be a great mistake, and so it was recently re-introduced.

The Grand Hotel in which we were staying in this hill station high up in the hills is probably not a lot different to what it was like in the 1920s at the height of the colonial days. There had been some modernization, like putting en suite facilities in the bedrooms, but the bar didn't look as if it had ever changed, and that Somerset Maugham characters were lurking in the corners waiting to re-inhabit their bar when we had gone to bed. These people were there, though, in old black and white photos hanging round the walls, which bore witness to the way of life of the privileged white man in those far-off days. While I was unpacking in my room, there was a knock at the door, and I answered to find a 45-year-old man in a smart white servant's suit who announced to me that he was my Boy (Boy!), and would it be convenient to turn down my bed. Nothing was too much trouble to make the guest's stay a happy one, and he spent ages doing this simple job as though it was a work of art.

The golf course nearby was even more steeped in Colonial history, with the corridors of the clubhouse and the changing rooms reminiscent of some of the older clubs I have visited in the UK. Over 100 years old, there is an air of faded gentility about the place which carried on to the golf course itself, with its fairways heavily lined with tall trees both coniferous and deciduous. To complete the picture, there were steep hills all round and with the low cloud and persistent drizzle, we could have been in, say, Scotland! The course itself was not in the best condition, as they had had a lot of rain and had been unable to cut the fairways, and putting was a lottery for the same reason. Despite the above, I really enjoyed playing this old course, and I would like to come back here and stay in the same hotel for three days and play golf without having to drive around so much. The temperature and climate is ideal for playing most of the time, and I think we were just a little unlucky.

The journey back to Negumbo, where we spent our last night, followed the road that we had come up on our way to Nuwara Eliya, but this time in daylight. It was cut into the hillside like a ribbon discarded from a child's Christmas present, and it did not look as if our bus would even fit on it, let alone negotiate it. Even so, the driver had to shunt round some of the hairpin bends – scary stuff! The hillsides were nearly vertical (or at least looked it), and every square inch was planted with tea bushes as far as you could see – but funnily enough we saw no-one at work. The higher you go, the better the tea, and as we descended the crops changed to vegetables being grown on terraces which were being sold at the side of the road, all as fresh and clean as you could have wanted them to be. Still further down there were dramatic waterfalls at the bottom of the valley, which we were able to see just before nightfall.

After a long and tiring bus ride, the last thing we needed was a detour when we were less than half-an-hour from the hotel, but that's what we got. Floods blocked our road, so we had to turn back and find another way. This new route took us over a bridge that looked no more than a foot wider than the bus, and judging by the amount of water rushing under it, was itself in danger of being swept away along with all of us!We spent a short night at the hotel, leaving at 4.30 a.m.to fly back to Bangkok, and at the airport we went through seemingly endless formalities before being allowed to visit the café at 6.30 only to find that it didn't open until 7.30, and our plane was due to take off at 7.40! Is this a legacy of British bureaucracy?

There was a general election in Sri Lanka while we were there, and there were lots of coloured flags out like bunting, as if it was the day of the annual village fete. Blue flags were for the ruling party of Mrs. Bandanaraike's daughter, green ones were out for the opposition, and just to make things more colourful, yellow flags signified the death of a Buddhist monk while white ones were for mourning Roman Catholics. We saw nothing of the Tamil separatists from the North; like matters in Ulster, apart from occasional outrages, the problems are confined to that area. Groups of Tamils emigrated from southern India some while ago, and feel that they are not, and do not want to be, part of Sri Lanka any more. The Colombo Government is fighting the election on throwing everything at the Tamils in order to bring them to heel, but the opposition wants to resolve the situation by negotiation. An escalating war is what the people want like they want a hole in the head, but choices like these are facing all civilized peoples in today's world.

CHAPTER 16

Singapore, October 2000

It was half term this week, which included two weekends, and we took the opportunity to take four days off to visit Singapore. So we booked rooms at the Hotel Rendezvous on Bras Basah road. The City State is on an island connected to Malaya by a single causeway across the River Salat Johor, and the view from the SAS plane as we approached at dusk was enchanting. All the skyscraper buildings were lit up, and the whole place had a fairy-tale appearance.

The taxi ride from Changi airport to the hotel was fast and efficient – as it all is in Singapore. It has a rather 'anti-septic' feel about it, where everything has its place, and nothing is allowed to interfere with the man-made order of things. Pedestrians and drivers all behave with great courtesy to one another, with traffic lights and crossings being observed punctiliously, because on-the-spot fines are regularly imposed on those who infringe the regulations. We were unaware of this, and jay-walked without penalty, because I suppose we weren't spotted by anyone in authority!

The first thing we did was to buy ourselves some good and inexpensive cameras. There seemed to be sales on in most shops, and the best sign that caught my eye was in a shoe shop where they were offering 'Buy One and Get One Free'!

The seafood here is quite amazing, and there are restaurants catering for every taste in the city. Although 70% of the population are of Chinese descent, there are many other ethnic groups, all of whom have their own specialist shops and food. In Bangkok, there are so many food outlets on the streets, cooking on gas or charcoal, but this is seemingly offensive in Singaporean eyes, and these small traders have been grouped together in specific places to cook and sell their different foods, so now they do not impede pedestrians with their chairs and tables and mobile barrows as they used to, and are nicely tucked away. The chairs and tables are in fact attached to the ground to stop them getting in a muddle, so order and efficiency permeates every aspect of life!

This was no more apparent than when we were on a guided bus tour of the island including a visit to Changi Gaol, taking in a mock-up Malay village on the way. The village was actually made of concrete and polystyrene, and though the houses and their settings with their clay models inside looked OK, there was absolutely no feel about the place. Perhaps it was because it was air-conditioned throughout, which of course it would never have been in real life – then or now. The most memorable thing in this village was that we were caught in the most almighty storm while (fortunately) we were inside, and I have to relate that while we were listening to the deafening claps of thunder overhead, an American woman looked out to see a flash of lightning. "My God," she exclaimed, "there's lightning out here as well!"

Changi Gaol itself was a little disappointing, as we were not allowed inside the prison compound, and had to look at the high walls and watchtowers from outside. There was a makeshift chapel which was made by the prisoners in 1940-41, but even that turned out to be a replica as the original had been taken away and re-erected in Melbourne or Sydney. The photographs and scrawled diaries of the inmates which are in the museum made up for this, and life under the Japanese in those far-off days became more of a reality.

That evening we took the 'Moonlight Safari' at the zoo in the north of the island, and spent two magical hours walking around floodlit compounds through dense jungle and concrete paths watching various animals following their nocturnal habits. Lights positioned high in the trees lit them up while probably not exposing us human animals to them at all. There were wolves, buffalo, rhinos, tigers, leopards, hyenas, otters, giraffe and several horned animals ranging from the size of a dog to that of a large horse, as well as many others, including snakes. We went into one netted compound, which we entered by going through two gates, in which were flying free many species of bats. Fruit bats, which have a wingspan of three or four feet, flew around in total silence before hanging upside down on a tree, near enough to touch, but of course we didn't do this because they were probably not only covered in fleas, but also their teeth looked extremely sharp!

The city was very relaxing to walk about in, as well as to sit and watch people, which we did on several occasions while sinking a beer in a pavement bar. Most of the main streets are tree lined, and so there is nearly always protection from the sun, which can be very hot in this latitude of two degrees north. (Bangkok is 14 degrees). We walked to Raffles Hotel where we had a Singapore Gin Sling in the Long Bar, which is where the colonial officers spent their off-duty hours in the days of the British Empire. The floor was covered with peanut shells, and it seems that it was customary for patrons to drop them after extracting the nuts. So of course we did the same, but walking on the floor was a bit like being on a shingle beach. Having said we had been to Raffles, we hadn't really; the hotel has had so many face-lifts over the years, that the Long Bar has long since disappeared, and the site of it has changed at least twice, and would be almost certainly unrecognizable by Somerset Maugham's characters of the 1920s and 30s.

The government here is what is called a controlled democracy, so practically everything that the citizens do is regulated by the State. There are fines for every anti-social activity and prison terms (often with caning as well) for more serious offences. For murder and drug offences the death penalty by hanging is still in force, and this may explain why there seems to be little crime. Mugging is virtually unheard of, and the streets at night are safe.

Changi airport is certainly the finest I have been in, and I think it is acknowledged to be one of the best in the world. With plenty of space and carpeted floors all over, it is more like a five-star hotel, and waiting for a plane is a real pleasure. When checking in to go home we were told that the plane was full, and we could not all sit together (Edward's friend Leo, a Singaporean, was with us), and would we mind two of us being up-graded? Well, no, we wouldn't mind really, and we had the most comfortable ride home making the most of their hospitality in business class. It made such a difference having our food brought to us course by course rather than everything together on a plastic tray, and drinking the (ad lib) wine out of proper wine glasses. We wobbled a bit as we left the plane!

It was a great few days, which gave us a glimpse of another part of South East Asia. Over 3,000,000 people live here, squashed in at the rate of 6,000 per square km, though it was not obvious that there was any crowding, as there are plenty of green spaces and parks, as well as the zoo and a nature reserve. Nearly everybody lives in high-rise accommodation, and most of the buildings are good to look at, and had been erected with regard to one another – quite unlike Bangkok. The traffic moves smoothly on good roads, and finally, although many languages are spoken here, the lingua franca is English and so we were understood and could understand wherever we were.

CHAPTER 17

Burma, October 2001

For a long time we had wanted to go to Burma, or Myanmar as it is known today, while we were here in South East Asia, and having overcome the question of whether we would be supporting a despotic regime or aiding the people, we settled on the latter and booked flights for half-term on October 2001. Then came the horrific event in New York on September 11, and we wondered if it was safe to fly anywhere at all as retribution might escalate to this part of the world. We decided to carry on, although the couple we were going with stayed in Bangkok, and just the three of us went. And very glad we were too.

A colony of Britain from 1852 until 1948, the country is now ruled by an un-elected military dictatorship. In 1990 the people had free elections, but the party which won, led by Aung San Suu Kyi, was not allowed to take their rightful seats in government, and in fact the leader herself was put under house arrest for six years. She is still not free to leave the country, and only has limited freedom in the country now – that is until she openly criticizes the government, or is perceived to do so. She was awarded the Nobel Peace Prize some years ago, but had she left the country to accept it, she would not have been allowed back in. A socialist or nearly communist state, the country is on its knees economically. A certain amount of private trading is allowed, though farmers and traders have to pay a high price for the privilege of doing so. This leads to a lot of deals under the counter and, like Thailand, officials line their pockets at public expense at every opportunity. Not a very attractive way of life, but seemingly endemic in this part of the world. The US dollar is the currency most preferred from abroad, and on arrival each person (in 2000) was obliged to buy $200 worth of Foreign Exchange Currency (FECs), and these can be used anywhere. There is no point in keeping any as they could not be exchanged back on departure. We had no trouble using them, as we paid all our hotel bills with them, but this is a real nuisance for people on a package tour who have paid for everything in advance.

The local currency is the kyat (pronounced chat) and the official exchange rate is six kyat to one dollar. However in the backstreets of Yangon (Rangoon) your guide can get from between 600 and 700 to the dollar – yes, 100 times more! On the first day we employed a guide with a car and driver (well actually they employed us by their perserverance, really), and after taking us to the hotel we had booked from Bangkok, took us off to change some money. I did not know the rate at the time, and gave him $200 which he hid in an old newspaper and went off, leaving us in the car with the driver. After nearly an hour, we were beginning to think that we were the victims of some sort of scam, and we were going to be dumped on the pavement in this little side street with no money at all, but the guide reappeared clutching a large brown envelope. In it he had K120,000 in 500 and 200 kyat notes, so there was much too much to fit into my wallet, and I had to keep it in the envelope. At these rates, K200 is about 25p, and I felt like a real cool operator peeling of wads of notes in the market! K10 is the smallest denomination, there are no coins, and all the notes are extremely scruffy, as you would expect.

In trying to rid themselves of any connection with the British, the name of the country was changed to Myanmar. The people however, are still Burmese and the official language is Burmese, but there are over 100 dialects in the country, though few of them are readily understood by one another. The legacy of the British influence is that most people understand and speak some English, which is most refreshing after living in Thailand where on the whole the people do not. When the British were here, the rule of the road was to drive on the left, so they changed that, but not the steering wheels of the cars – even the new ones, so the driver is in the gutter. They cannot see round a lorry properly for overtaking – but go anyway, which is most unnerving for the front seat passenger, which was usually me. On many occasions I shut my eyes as we appeared to be playing 'chicken' with oncoming vehicles!

Our guide took us to a number of places in Yangon, but what stood out was the Schwedagon Pagoda. A Buddhist shrine which was in existence before the eleventh century, it has constantly been renovated and added to ever since, and is now a remarkable place of pilgrimage. The pagoda houses a casket containing eight hairs from the head of the Lord Buddha, and on the long journey from India, two of them got lost and two of them got stolen, but when the casket arrived in Yangon, they found all eight of them inside: a miracle, so it is a very holy place. Round the central pagoda were small statues of the seated Buddha, each surrounded by a trough of water, and dedicated to a different day of the week. The merit-making custom is to pour one small cup of water for each year of your life over the head of the Buddha which represents the day of the week that you were born. First Bridget did this, then Eddy and I, but they both finished much more quickly than I did, as it seemed to take for ever, even though I was using both hands! The difficult thing here is to keep your feet cool. As with all holy places, you are required to go barefoot, and with the hot sun blazing down on to the marble flooring, we found ourselves scampering about from shadow to shadow to find a shady spot to stand in and wonder at the beauty of the place. And it was all well worth the effort.

We spent some time here, and then we were taken to the old wharf area which is a complete contrast, where we might have gone back 150 years to Dickensian times. Apart from the ancient lorries and some equally ancient small boats with outboard motors, there was not a machine in sight – not a crane, not a forklift and not even a sack barrow to be seen. Men were walking to and fro over a gang plank with 75 to 100 kg sacks on their backs (each sack was too heavy to lift, and it needed two men to load one on to the back of a third). What they were carrying I have no idea, probably agricultural produce, but it may well have been illegal drugs for all I know. There were several boats lined up on the quayside and others were unloading oil drums and back loading empties. Amongst all this bustle were foot passengers carrying babies and bundles, some with two baskets balancing on a pole over their shoulder, taking their produce to market somewhere, I suppose.

And you couldn't put your foot down anywhere without treading on a bright crimson splat from the juice of the betel nut, which a great number of people chew and spit. This is the case all over the country and you see many people – both men and women – with bright red lips and rotting teeth. This is the least charming of Burmese customs, but a much more endearing one is that of putting a yellow paste on their cheeks. Made from the bark of the thanaka tree, it is ground into a paste with water and mainly used by young women. Partly as an adornment and partly as protection from the sun, it is said to keep young skin taut into old age, though there was a singular lack of evidence of this among the older women we encountered! Bridget was given some on her arm and it had a cooling effect as well. The young girls do not just slap it on their faces but take the trouble to make patterns of squares or circles.

Back in Yangon, we left the wharf area to its own busy life of hawkers, beggars, workers and general layabouts, apparently making no effort to get into the twentieth century, let alone the twenty-first. From there we went to the Strand Hotel, which was built at the end of the nineteenth century for the servants of the British Crown, and is very similar to Raffles in Singapore and became their social centre. This hotel is one of the few places in Yangon, if not Burma as a whole, that have had any sort of renovation, but it still has the air of faded opulence one associates with the remnants of the British Empire. Everywhere we looked, even at some of the holy places, the faces of buildings were crumbling and plaster was falling off. Rainwater from leaking gutters has made dark green marks down the walls (inside as well, I expect), and plants can be seen growing in the mortar between the bricks. Generally speaking, the infrastructure of the country appeared to be at a very low level. The electricity supply in Yangon is cut off from 10 a.m. until 4 p.m. every day, but everyone has their own generator as a source of power for these times, consequently while we were walking up the street one day at 10 a.m, a cacophony of two-stroke engines started up as, of course, all the shops had their own generators on the pavement!

That evening we went for a walk, having supper in (of all places) a Thai restaurant, before finding our way into a street market. Nearly all the men wear a longyi rather than trousers, and this is a piece of cloth about two metres long which wraps round the waist rather like a bath towel. I bought a cotton one for very little money, but was quite unable to make it stay up as I couldn't figure out how to fold it properly. I looked pretty stupid in it, anyway, so I was not all that keen on wearing it! During this walk, I was followed for about 20 minutes by a beggar woman who was suckling a baby at her breast. She kept nudging me and holding out her hand, and I became increasingly embarrassed by the thought that to her my pockets were filled with unimaginable wealth. But I had become immune to the beggars of Bangkok who are largely run by mafia gangs, so I gave her nothing which, in retrospect, I regretted.

The security for all flights, including domestic, is quite high nowadays and we had to present our passports to be inspected regularly, but we eventually arrived in Heho which is the airport nearest to Inle Lake, our destination. We were met, and driven for 45 minutes along twisting, sometimes dirt, roads full of potholes at high speed. Coasting downhill is pretty hairy, but saves petrol (which is expensive here), and we arrived in one piece to find that we were the only guests at the resort. We had been given a chalet with three beds overlooking the lake, and arriving in the late afternoon we were able to sit on our verandah and observe the peaceful scene until dusk gave way to night.

Next day we had arranged for a boat with a knowledgeable boatman to show us the lake. There are villages on stilts all round the edge and also many on it, as it is only about ten feet deep at the most. Our first stop after an hour was a market, and as there was no quay, we had to disembark by climbing over other boats on to the muddy shore. There had been some heavy rain the night before, and the whole place was pretty muddy, but we walked around on duckboards. We were accosted on all sides, there being no other tourists in sight, to buy 'antiques' which were a 'special price', or were 'cheaper in the morning'. We bought two or three little wooden items which may or may not have been made 200 years ago (yesterday?), but they were pleasing to the eye, and definitely not tacky souvenirs. Further into the market were all the mundane necessities for life, like food and furniture and the narrow walkways were teeming with people. Round the back I spotted a car park – except it wasn't for cars: it was full of ox-carts, some of which had one patient animal in the shafts, and others had two. There were a number of pony carts as well, and the whole place was ankle deep in mud.

There is a lot of cottage industry on the lake, and visitors are more than welcome to look round the inhabitants' premises and their work, and perhaps buy something although there was no pressure to do so. We found that the Burmese people everywhere we went were more friendly than the Thais (and even more so than the Chinese). Perhaps this was because as tourists we only see life on the surface, and it was like going back to how I imagine life was like in the UK 100 years or more ago. We visited a silk-weaving factory where there must have been 100 looms on three floors in two buildings, all clattering away to the sound of flying shuttles. The pedals of the looms were worked by the operator's bare feet, and the shuttle propelled by a sharp tug on a stick attached to some ropes. They were weaving some complicated and beautiful patterns and everyone – nearly all girls – looked happy in their work.

Our next visit was most unlikely – a forge. This was in a building on stilts with a wooden floor and rush mat walls and roof, and was, I would have thought, a severe fire hazard, but this did not seem to matter. They were not there for shoeing hooves, as the ponies we saw had none, and anyway it would be difficult to get them here over the water. They were making agricultural implements, and today they were making brishing hooks, or sickles. One man took hot iron from the fire and put it on an anvil, whereupon four strong young men wielding 10lb hammers rhythmically rained blows on it until the boss was satisfied. The forced air to the fire was operated by a boy who was standing astride two tubes containing the bellows, and he pumped down alternately with each leg to provide the air. His rest time came while his colleagues were hammering, and their rest time was when he was pumping. We bought nothing here, but we were given tea by the family and we gave the children exercise books and pens, of which we had brought a good supply, because we had been told they were in great demand here. They were so grateful, and it is sad that the education of children is so neglected.

The neighbouring factory produced cigars. Nine young girls sat cross-legged in three rows of three with a large basket of tobacco in front of each of them. Deftly, they rolled the loose tobacco inside a single leaf, but not, I am sorry to say, on their bare thighs! Another illusion shattered. The tobacco gives a very mild smoke and I bought a box of 20, and when I asked to buy a few more, they gave me a handful with a charming smile and no charge.

There is a story that many years ago, when five Buddha heads were being transported across the lake to a temple, the boat overturned in a squall. The boatmen searched and searched for them but could only find four. When they eventually arrived at the temple, they found the fifth one already there: a miracle, So this place is very holy, and devout Buddhists come here on a pilgrimage to put little squares of gold leaf on the heads of the statues. This is a very common practice for Buddhists to 'make merit', and these small gold leaf patches are on sale for a few pence each. There have been so many stuck on these particular heads, that they are virtually featureless. I bought a small packet of patches, and while Bridget and Eddy looked on, I did my stuff with everyone else, though I felt a little uncomfortable amongst the devotees.

The outstanding peculiarity of the lake is the floating farms. These are extremely fertile beds which are formed first by collecting the weed water-hyacinth and matting it together so that it can be anchored to the bottom of the lake with bamboo poles. Then silt is dredged from the bottom by hand and dumped on these floating pontoons to a depth of about two feet, and after two crops it is allowed to sink, and another one is made. We saw acres and acres of tomatoes as well as cucumbers, cabbages, cauliflowers and many other crops, all looking extremely healthy. Husbandry was carried out from small boats which moved up and down the narrow waterways between the beds, and so there was no compaction of the soil at all – not even from footsteps. Planting and harvesting went on all the year round, and we saw crops and beds in all stages of production and preparation. Seeing the beds undulating in the wash from our boat gave them an unreal appearance, as though they were staggering about in a drunken manner.

Another feature of the lake is the way the fishermen propel their boats along. They stand precariously on one foot on the stern of their narrow, shallow and fragile boats made from hollowed out tree trunks. By using the heel of the other foot and one hand on the single oar they control the speed and direction of the boat, leaving the other hand to cast a line or net into the water. By standing up they have a much better view of where the fish are, and have a large conical net in the shape of a funnel, which is the traditional and most efficient way of catching fish. It all looks most ungainly, but they've been doing it for hundreds of years, and it works very well in these shallow waters.

All around the lake are ramshackle dwellings made of woven bamboo that are side by side with larger ones made more substantially of wood. Early in the morning of the next day, our boat went through some very narrow channels to get to the villages, and on several occasions the boatman had to push us off the floating side banks with his oar, while we just hoped that we wouldn't have to get off and push! There were not many tourists out early in the day – in fact it is a little early in the year for them as well – and many people stopped what they were doing and lined their houses to wave to us. Another indication of how friendly the people are.

We were on our way to Nyaungshure at the north end of the lake, having been south the day before. We disembarked across a wobbly plank and spent an hour in the town where they were getting ready for an annual festival. Several streets were closed, and they were putting up temporary shelters for street traders out of bamboo canes and rush matting. Some of them were already in business, and it was at one of these that a stall holder gave Bridget some yellow paste made from the bark of the thanaka tree, and spread it on her arm.

Back at the hotel, we spent a very peaceful two hours on our verandah reflecting on the tranquillity of the lake. The only noise was the cry of the water birds, and the pop-popping of the small motor boat engines in the distance. The lake, being 3,000 feet above sea level, has a freshness in the air which is not found at lower altitudes and we were sad to leave this place which I would recommend for a week of complete relaxation. We came back to the real world when our taxi took us back to Heho in another nerve-wracking drive. At the airport our bags were physically searched for dangerous objects as they had no x-ray machines – one has become so accustomed to there being an array of sophisticated equipment at airports, that this search came as quite a surprise.

We were met in Mandalay by Win, a guide arranged by a friend in Bangkok, and he had booked us into a hotel. After supper he took us to a marionette theatre for an hour of traditional puppetry with stories from the history and culture of Burma. It was accompanied by a five-piece band of mainly percussion: of gongs, wood blocks and drums and a reed instrument which was rather like an oboe. This played what passed for (I suppose) a melody in a high-pitched squeak, and we were totally entranced by the performance, having gone to the theatre with a great deal of misgiving. This ancient art was a favourite entertainment of kings and queens, and people looked forward to a visit by the troupe as one might look forward to a rock star's concert nowadays. The curtain rose up from time to time to show the puppeteers at work, which was fascinating, and the one-hour show was just the right length.

Beggars and hawkers are the blight of Mandalay – they will not leave you alone. If you give them anything, and we had plenty of pens to give to children, they swarm around you wanting (even demanding) more. We had to be quite forceful in getting rid of them by being verbally explicit. However, having said that, a couple of students attached themselves to us while walking round a temple without our guide, and while practising their English, were very useful guides, so we tipped well.

We were plagued by them when we went for a walk on the famous teak bridge over a lake, which rather spoilt our visit. The U Bein Bridge is a rather scary walkway of nearly one mile much of which has no side rails; bicycles whizz up and down, and this made us feel rather vulnerable, so we only went half way. Although 25 feet above the water, the lake is only waist deep, and there were many people fishing from the bridge as well as in the water. Had we been pushed or fallen off, no great harm would have come to us other than getting snagged by a fish hook on the way down!

Nearby is the Mahaungmye Monastery, which we visited. The monks have their main meal of the day at about 10.30 in the morning, and here they line up for their food and all eat together in the refectory. There are up to 1,000 of them in absolute silence except for the scraping of plates. This is quite amazing when you think of the cacophony in the dining hall at school with less than half that number! People were moving up and down the rows of tables with cameras, and I felt intrusive doing so, but I did take one or two discreet snaps of the general scene.

On the way back to Mandalay, we stopped by the riverside where teak logs had been rafted down from the north and were being loaded on to road vehicles. Young water buffaloes hauled the logs to the water's edge when older and more experienced animals took over. They dragged each log to an ancient lorry, and pushed them up a ramp until they overbalanced on to the floor, and then they backed up a bit and pushed them forward until they were up against the headboard of the lorry. All this was done with the minimal of grunts from their driver. It was all very orderly, and while time did not actually stand still, it seemed to be going on in very slow motion.

In the evening we took a tri-shaw ride to a Shan restaurant. A tri-shaw is a tricycle with a sidecar that has two seats – one facing forward, and the other back – and not a means of transport that I would recommend to anyone. I am a little wider than the average Burmese, so was not particularly comfortable in the eight-mile tour we had of the city at night after supper. Not only that, but it was most unnerving that the street lighting (where there was any) was very poor and the tri-shaw had no lights, but also it seemed that it was at the discretion of car drivers to use their lights as well. Thus, at crossroads there was no really certain way of knowing whether a car was coasting (to save petrol) towards you or not. This was all rather hairy.

The meal which we had before this was the local food from the Shan division of Burma. The Union of Burma was made up by the British from a collection of States who were at peace with one another for periods, and waging bitter wars in between, and they all have their own customs and food specialities. Shan food is less bland than some of the food we have had here, but not as spicy as Thai. On the whole we found the food not particularly memorable, nor the beer. Mandalay rum with coke was an excellent drink, however.

The gold leaf that Buddhists paste on their idols is hammered out by hand. We watched while workers pounded small blocks of gold placed between foil and wrapped in a deer hide package. They beat each package for a total of six hours, moving it around every six minutes so that it becomes evenly beaten, and they time this with a coconut shell floating in water that has a hole in it, and when the shell sinks, it is time to turn the package again. A European tried to introduce a machine for this arduous and repetitive work, but the quality of the finished article was inferior, so they scrapped it. Anyway, although the beaters are paid very poorly, they get a lot of merit for doing this holy work, and there is no shortage of workers to do it. Making merit in this, or any other way, ensures a better station in the next life, and you may come back as one who gives orders rather than receives them. This is what keeps the under-privileged happy in Buddhist countries – the rich, too, for fear of a lower status.

We steamed up the Ayeyarwadi (Irrawaddy) river for about an hour to Mingun to see an old temple that was damaged by an earthquake 150 years ago while it was being built; it was never finished, but never fell down either, although there is a great crack across the face. Bridget and Eddy climbed to the top while I enjoyed a beer in the shade at the bottom! In the village there is a 90-ton bell which hangs two feet off the ground supported by an enormous shackle from two heavy RSJs. It is said to be the largest bell in the world, and when I hit it with a piece of wood (hanging nearby for the purpose) it gave a most sonorous ring which was very pleasing to the ear.

During the journey upstream, there was a young man towing a sail boat from the bank at the same speed as we were going. He was trudging over sand and mud and through waist-deep water, all the while smoking a cigar. I can't imagine what sort of fare he was being paid for this, but I can only think that he was pleased to have a job of any sort, and all the while I think that his employer in the boat was fast asleep!

Mandalay Hill is the place to be at sunset, so we made our way up the hairpin bends until nearly at the top; the last bit is by lift, escalator or steps. We were obliged to take the steps because a 'big-wig' had indicated that he wanted to go up this evening and so lift and elevator were closed in case he turned up. He didn't, but this is how the country is run, and status is everything, although in this 'socialist' state it is surprising to find that some people are more equal than others. 'Twas ever thus. But we forgot all that as the sun went down over the distant hills, reflected in the waters of the great river. It has been described as one of the most romantic experiences, and I can certainly vouch for that. It provided a memorable finale for our visit to Mandalay. In fact Mandalay is a pretty memorable place altogether, with its fine teak buildings with intricate carving, not to mention the Kathodaw Pagoda which houses the largest book of its kind in the world (so they say). It contains 729 pages, each inscribed on marble and each double page is housed in a small pagoda of its own, all situated around the central pagoda.

Leaving Mandalay was a bit of a farce. The summary of our flights given to us by the travel agent showed that our flight to Bagan was at 12.50, but there was nothing doing at the airport, and when I checked on the ticket, it said quite clearly 17.05. Fortunately not the other way round, there was nothing for it but to wait for four hours in the airport. There was a decent restaurant, so our time was not wasted too badly. We were the only people in this vast cavernous airport which is only open at the moment for domestic flights. It has facilities for handling five jumbo jets at once, and our little 100-seater turbo jet looked like a toy on the enormous apron.

Arriving at our hotel in Bagan, we found we had been given a small chalet with three beds in it. This whole room could have been fitted into the lobby of our really spacious room in Mandalay, where there was so much room that Eddy was able to play with his football! So we had to undress and do our ablutions separately, but we are not complaining as none of our rooms have cost more than US$40 for bed and breakfast, and this one was $30, and we are not here for the luxury.

After a hot and sunny three days in Mandalay, we were woken up by rain crashing down on the tin roof of our chalet. Unfortunately the clouds remained, with drizzle for the two days we were here, but we got up at 5 a.m. the next morning anyway to climb one of the thousands of pagodas here to see the sunrise. All we saw was the light going from black to grey at around 6.30! Bagan is a truly remarkable place. It is an area of about 40 km^2, and small pagodas abound, largely built by kings who wished to atone for something or to make merit. Mostly built in the eleventh and twelfth centuries at the same time as the great cathedrals in Europe, they were all built in this small area, and for the last two centuries left to rot. And many of them are dangerous to visit on account of the crumbling fabric. We went through the same performance at 5.30 to see the sunset, with the same result! The climb on this one was most difficult, as the steps had 6" treads and 24" risers which I negotiated by using both hands and feet. Coming down was much more of problem, but fortunately there was a stout handrail.

In the Dhammayangyi Temple we saw a reminder of the barbarity of past times. There was a flat stone on the floor with the indentation of a cross cut into it; the king used to visit the temple while it was being built and he carried with him a needle. The bricks and stones had to fit on one another so perfectly, that if he could push this needle easily between the joints, then the mortar must be too weak and the worker responsible would be held down over this stone with his arm over the indentations while another worker chopped his hand off. Ugh!

Two hours' drive from Bagan is Mount Popa, a 250,000-year-old extinct volcano. On top is perched a monastry which is reached by a climb of 777 steps from the village where we parked the car after another adventurous drive up the hillside with our guide Po. I sat in a café with a beer while Bridget and Eddy climbed up to the monastery where they saw only a fairly good view, having been besieged by beggars and hawkers all the way up and down. I was unmolested and watched life in the village street which, after the previous night's rain, was a quagmire of mud. Amongst the humans lived a troupe of monkeys who were grabbing morsels of food from anyone they could, and being quite aggressive to people carrying bags of food home from the market. Fortunately, they didn't come near me, but they can be a terrible nuisance even though their antics can be quite amusing.

On the way, we visited a farmer who produced oil from sesame seeds and peanuts. We were greeted in a very friendly fashion with cups of tea by this relatively well-off family – you could see this, we were told by the ox they had walking round and round grinding the peanuts into oil. The poorer farmers do this by hand. Being ignorant of peanut farming, I was surprised to see them growing on roots underground. The farmer lifted a plant to show me, and then replanted it easily in this lovely friable and fertile volcanic soil which was in a lovely condition even after heavy rain. He gave us some of the liquor that they made from the palm oil (the toddy palm) which tasted rather like schnapps, but less alcoholic. Then he shinned up a tree of about 50 feet and maybe 70 to 80 years old to show us how the oil was harvested, not up the trunk in bare feet, but up a rickety fixed ladder made of bamboo and coconut string. Rather him than me!

Back in Yangon for our final day we spent quite a bit of time in the Bogyoke (or Scott) market where we got rid of our remaining cash which we were unable to take out of the country with us. A large covered area of two-storey buildings and walkways there are shops and stalls here to cater for all tastes and pockets. The prime sites in the middle of the market are occupied by jewellers, all bearing the legend 'Government Approved'. If you are dead set on buying gems, you should get them here and get a proper receipt and provenance for them, but on the other hand, being government approved means that it is government owned, and the state takes the profits.

On the plane going home, Bridget became uncontrollably shivery, and worried that she might have caught malaria, which has flu-like symptoms; after a bad night's sleep we went to the doctor the next day who diagnosed a virulent strain of food poisoning after taking blood tests. We were all very thankful that this didn't happen during our stay, as it so easily could have done. It was probably caused by a Baman (another division of Burma) meal we had in Bagan the day before. They bring to your table about 20 different small dishes, and you help yourself to a bed of rice and then add whatever takes your fancy. Pork, chicken, mutton, beef, fish, all sorts of vegetables, some curried, some not, some spicy, some not. As you empty one dish, they refill it until you have had enough, and then probably empty what's left back into the parent dish on the hob, though we didn't see this. By far the most tasty food we had in Burma, this must have been where Bridget, and to a lesser extent Eddy, got their bugs from. I, on the other hand, am far less adventurous with food, and having tasted a dish of what looked like whitebait, I stuck with it to the exclusion of others, and wasn't ill at all.

Burma is a very green country inhabited by very friendly people, who on the whole are very poor. Schools are available to all from six to 16, but colleges and universities were closed down in 1996 because the government is afraid of student uprisings. There are a limited number of colleges for specific professions such as medicine and teaching, but they are only available to those whose families can afford the fees. While monasteries provide much of the primary education, they are only able to afford one free one in Yangon, where presumably devout Buddhists would not dream of demonstrating against the government.

One of Burma's main sources of income is the manufacture and export of illegal drugs, much of it across the Thai border. The Burmese pay lip service to an agreement to stamp it out, but don't do too much about it, and millions of pounds worth are exported annually leading to military scuffles on the border from time to time. But corruption is endemic in this part of the world, and those in power on both sides are skimming too much off the top for themselves to put their hearts and minds into stopping this lucrative trade.

The brutal way in which the government keeps the lid on anti-government discussion results in many arrests and incarceration without trial. We did not attempt to talk politics to anyone, not even in the privacy of the car with our guide – we may have just have been talking to the wrong person – so we don't really know what the grass roots feelings are. But we do suspect that they would overthrow this non-democratic junta if they could.

I have said little of Aung San Suu Kyi, the leader of the National League for Democracy, who was awarded the Nobel Peace Prize but never allowed out of the country to collect it. In 1990, in a parliamentary election which the junta thought they had rigged, she won 80% of the vote, but the junta quashed the result and have kept 'The Lady', as she is known, either in prison or house arrest ever since, except for a short period in 2002. The junta, or clique, which calls itself the State Peace and Development Council has committed nearly every conceivable abuse against its people and country. With the collusion of China and certain elements of the Thai military they are stripping gem mines and teak forests as well as trafficking in opiates. In a country which has such fertile soil, one third of the children are undernourished, and AIDS flourishes. The government continually rejects any sort of help or interference from abroad, and it is difficult to know where it will all end. But a most delightful people living in a beautiful land surely cannot be suppressed for ever, and one can only hope that democracy will come about by peaceful rather than violent means.

CHAPTER 18

Hong Kong, October 2002

Three or four months ago we were playing an annual golf match against another society for the 'Emirates' Cup, and I hadn't realised until this year that it was sponsored by the airline, who are very generous with their prizes. Apart from presenting the cup, they also give 'long drive' and 'near pin' prizes, and Bridget won a return flight to Hong Kong for a near pin. Worth about 120 pounds (does this make her a professional?) I bought my own ticket, and we went off at the first opportunity, which was half term in October.

At the check-in Bridget was offered – as a VIP guest – an upgrade to business class, which she accepted. I could have one if I paid extra, and although there were plenty of business class seats, they would not allow me even to visit her. It was only for two hours, and I had a window seat and no one next to me, so that was OK. I had my camera at the ready as we flew in, but the clouds were so dense and low that I could barely see the wingtip let alone a fabulous view of the city below.

Before we got off the ground, however, Bridget had to be allowed out of the country. Because she still had some unpaid tax (see page 47), which, in Bridget's case was about 240,000 baht (4,000 pounds) including the penalty for not paying on time. The school was trying to sort it out, but in the meantime Bridget's passport had a black mark against it in the computer, and she had to be interrogated by immigration officials each time she wanted to leave the country. A Thai administrator from school came with us to the airport and was there to sort out any problem, and we got away all right.

The journey from Hong Kong's spacious airport was along a spanking new dual carriageway, and we were able to see the cramped conditions in which people lived in 30-storey apartment blocks huddling cheek by jowl with one another with hardly enough room to swing the proverbial cat between them. Very depressing up close, but from a distance they have a certain visual appeal – to the casual observer, anyway.

Once off the expressway, we travelled in the most convoluted way along a myriad of one-way streets until we got to The Kimberly Hotel in Kimberly Road, very close to Kowloon Park. Given a room on the ninth floor overlooking a building site, we were a bit surprised to find how short the lift journey was until we found out that the ninth floor was only four floors above ground level. Our stay was too short for us to spend any time working this one out! To our shame, our first culinary experience in the city was a bag of crisps to go with the whisky we had bought in the airport, and these we consumed with the complimentary basket of fruit we found in our room.

We awoke next morning to steady rain, so we set off for the Science Museum nearby only to find it closed for the morning. Opposite, however, was the Museum of Hong Kong, and it was free, so it must have been ordained that we should find ourselves here on our first day, because it was one of the best museums I have ever been in. The colony's history from pre-historic to post-colonial was set out and displayed with well designed exhibits, which were backed up with short video films in English, Chinese and many other languages.

I was unaware that Hong Kong's existence was based on the opium trade, and that the British were the outrageous 'baddies' in the opium wars of the nineteenth century. They imported opium from India to try to redress the serious imbalance of trade caused by the Chinese not wanting any British goods in exchange for their silks and spices. This trade however was so successful that the Emperor sent a special envoy to the area to stamp out its use, and to begin with he did very well. But when the British brought their military might to bear, the Chinese gave in and the very one-sided treaty of Nanking was signed whereby first Hong Kong Island, then Kowloon and then the New Territories were ceded to Britain for 100 years. Having reverted to China in 1997, it was now five years since Britain had control, and the history in the museum may have been a little biased towards the Chinese point of view!

There is, though, a strong British feel about the place. All the signposts and street names are in Chinese and English, and we met no one in the city who couldn't speak at least a little English, though this was not so in the countryside in the villages in the New Territories where not so many tourists venture. And the people are so friendly and helpful, quite unlike those in Beijing who were not only unfriendly, but downright rude on occasions. We were standing on a corner consulting a map when a local man came up to help us speaking in halting English, and we were almost sorry to have resolved the problem of our whereabouts by the time he got to us.

The Southern end of Nathan Road is known as the Golden Mile, and you can hardly move for people, most of whom are going the other way seemingly, and to compound this there are major road works going on which made the pavement half-width in many places. Outside every shop doorway there are touts trying to sell watches, jewellery, cameras, radios and all sorts of merchandise, and once in conversation it is difficult to get out. We asked the price of a small radio and the salesman said HK$ 500 (40 pounds). "Too much," I said. "How much then?" he said and not wanting anything really, I said "$250." "O.K." he said! Well, I managed to get out of it feeling rather foolish, but it does indicate to what extent tourists can be ripped off, and judging by the number of touts for instant tailoring services, there must be more tailors here than in Bangkok, which is saying something!

We had to run this gauntlet several times as this was our route to the harbour and the underground station (MTR), and that evening we were off to the Intercontinental Hotel on the waterfront. We had been told that we must sample the cocktails in the lounge without looking at the price list first. As the light faded and the waterfront lights came on, we sat in sumptuous surroundings with sumptuous cocktails looking at a sumptuous view, and eventually we had to settle a sumptuous bill! This is all part of life's rich pattern, I suppose. We followed this with rather a disappointing Cantonese meal served up in very atmospheric surroundings. Chosen out of the guide book, it was not a great success, and the next day we had a Shenzou meal, but that was not great either. I think that after Bangkok the food here is rather bland, and I am getting used to it being more spicy nowadays.

On our way home, we passed a shop whose window was full of Chinese ailment remedies, each of which was labelled and what ailment it was said to cure. There were animal, mineral as well as herbal cures for everything, from sore limbs, indigestion, impotence, flatulence and nocturnal emissions (whatever they are) to headaches, liver complaints and incontinence. I wouldn't know where to start – I think I need a bit of everything! I wonder whether I could get a franchise to open up in the professional's shop at my golf club in the UK – there could be a huge market here!

The Star Ferry has been constantly crossing and re-crossing the harbour every ten minutes or so between Hong Kong Island and Kowloon ever since it was started in 1888, and the shape of the ferries has hardly altered – if at all. They are regularly replaced, of course, but the design doesn't change which looks awfully top heavy, but one is greatly reassured to be told that they have an impeccable safety record. There are four or five tunnels, but that is a very un-romantic way to cross the harbour, and anyway the fare was only 20p for Bridget while OAPs were free.

Our objective today was Victoria Peak, the high point of Hong Kong Island from which you get a 360 degree view of the city and harbour. As we got on the wrong ferry at Kowloon, we arrived at Wanchai rather than Central, and before we realized that it was me that was wrong and not the map we wandered about like headless chickens. We had rather a hot walk to get to the Peak Tramway, and we stopped for coffee at the five-star Conrad Hotel on the way, and the cost of the coffee was easily offset by the quality of the people-watching that we did there, and my goodness, how the other half live when they are away from home!

There is a road up to the Peak, but the best way up the slope, which is one in three in places, is by the cable-operated funicular tramway. All the seats face uphill, as you would get pitched out of them if they were facing downhill, and an optical illusion occurs as the carriage goes between the high rise buildings, which makes them appear as if they are falling over while the tram is on the level. Most weird!

The views up here are quite spectacular though on looking out to sea we could only see a few islands as it was quite hazy, but the buildings of Hong Kong Island and Kowloon made an impressive backdrop to the harbour which is in between. Expecting to find only tacky souvenir stalls at the top, we did find them, but also there was a superior shopping mall and restaurants catering for proper meals as well as take-away. Fearing the worst, we bought sandwiches at the bottom which we consumed while admiring the view. There was a lot of work going on down below in the harbour, and I overheard a man from the North of England telling his wife that the authorities were always reclaiming land by tipping rubble into the harbour. We enjoyed her reply that " the trouble with doing that was the sea just kept on getting fuller." Irrefutable logic!

Stanley is a town on the south-east corner of Hong Kong Island, and it has a street market that we were told we should visit, so we took a taxi from the bottom station of the tramway and drove through some rugged scenery over some tortuous roads passing some gorgeous beaches on the way. The market is like many in Bangkok, sprawling over many streets, and we found it easy to lose our sense of direction, passing the same stalls from the other direction without realizing that we had turned round! We found nothing to take away except the experience, and got the bus back, which was not only one fifth of the taxi fare but from the top deck we had a fine view of the coast. That evening we found a restaurant serving Szechuan food which was much more tasty, though the difficulty I had eating a crab with chopsticks was solved by using my fingers.

We visited the New Territories the next day, and we hadn't realised that there were any rural parts to Hong Kong, we just thought it was a concrete jungle all the way from the sea to the Chinese border, but no. We started by getting the underground train from Tsim Sha Tsui and going to the end of the line at Tseun Wan, then by bus to Yeun Long and finally by taxi to Kam Tin. Kam Tin is one of the famous walled villages, and was founded 700 years ago by the Tong family to get away from and defend themselves from the lawless brigands in Shenzheu Province. It is remarkably small, and everyone who lives there bears the name of Tong. Walking through a doorway with an ironwork lattice gate into the village we found the streets only wide enough for a bicycle or a donkey, rather like the hutongs of Beijing. Most of the houses were original, but some had been modernized and some replaced with five storeys, with modern brickwork. Fascinating, but after ten minutes we had really seen all there was to see. The wall was intact all the way round, with just the one entrance and a castellated tower in one corner. I took a photo of an old crone who appeared to be asleep on her chair outside her house in the shade of the sun. I think the flash must have woken her up, because she suddenly sprang out of her chair crying blue murder at me as I retreated in great haste round a corner! Why was this? Had the photo removed part of her soul? or should I have given her some money? I'll never know, but I suspect the latter.

We caught a bus a little bigger than a minibus back to Yeun Long, and the driver stopped at some traffic lights alongside a colleague. Suddenly, our driver started revving his engine, and the other guy, thinking he was being challenged to a race, let in his clutch nearly doing a wheelie, and shot off through the still red lights giving all his passengers whiplash, while we waited for the green. Our driver and the rest of the bus were convulsed with laughter, including ourselves! This only goes to show that a good joke can cross both linguistic and cultural barriers with ease.

There is a charming residence at San Tin called Thai Fu Thai, and was built some 200 years ago by a senior bureaucrat of the Quing dynasty. Extremely simple in design, it is decorated in the most sophisticated manner, and is a most elegant building. The village in which it stands is small and also quite charming, but it is completely surrounded by industrial units and container depots because the area is served with some excellent roads. The lorries can't get into the village itself as the roads are too narrow, and it is possible to imagine the tranquillity that would have been there in days gone by. We stopped for refreshment at a small café and the proprietor came out and said his menu was all in Chinese, so he reeled off what he could do for us. He had been born in this village but had spent many years in London, though we were not quite clear whether he intended to remain here or not. He brought me out an enormous plate of fried noodles and chicken, and for Bridget a large bowl of noodle soup. I couldn't finish mine, and for two pounds we were extremely well looked after.

We continued back to Hong Kong by bus, and from the road we had some very good views of two of the most impressive bridges linking the city to the new airport on Lantan Island by way of T'sing Yi Island. The old airport which is in the middle of Kowloon had jumbo jets flying between tower blocks on their descent to the runway, which extended into the harbour. I knew a pilot who described it as one of the more interesting places to land – I think he meant frightening really! And whatever did first-time visitors think? Or did they have their eyes shut? Maybe the cabin staff pulled the window blinds down before landing, though this is, of course, unlikely.

A trip round the harbour at night with as many drinks as you wanted on board seemed a good idea, so we bought two tickets and arrived at Kowloon pier in plenty of time, but found no one else who was going on this trip.All the other passengers were from Hong Kong Island, and the boat turned up and stopped for two minutes only, and we were quite lucky not to be left behind. The promenade area from the Star Ferry pier to the Intercontinental Hotel has only been completed in the last few years. It is a wide pedestrian area on two levels with the old Clock Tower as a feature from the past, while the Art Museum, Space Museum and Cultural Centre represent the future. This last has been described as the largest and ugliest building without windows in the world. True, it has no windows, but not true that it is ugly – the walls soar upwards leaning in slightly from the perpendicular and it is topped by a roof with the most elegant sweep to it. At night it is floodlit in three colours and is a delightful feature of the harbour.

But back to the 'booze cruise' on which we downed several glasses of whisky each while watching the waterfront lights slip by, which became more magical by the minute (or should I say by the glass?). We steamed quite close to the runway of the old airport, and it must have been truly terrifying for a pilot to see nothing but water in front of him if he overshot. Part of it is now a golf driving range, and when they have cleared all the spilt fuel off the runway, it will be used for more housing. Walking back to the hotel quite late, we encountered the hustle and bustle of city night life, which feeds on itself to get the adrenaline flowing. We took our time to take it all in; it is a little different to Bangkok, where the accent is fairly heavily weighted towards the sex industry at night.

We did no shopping on Hong Kong Island – only window shopping – as this is the 'Knightsbridge' end of the city, and things were pretty expensive. What we could afford was a tram ride, and I really enjoyed this noisy, smelly and uncomfortable ride through the city streets squashed up against members of the public (we had to stand). I kept my hand firmly on my wallet and Bridget her bag, as we were obvious and easy targets for pick-pockets. Having had my pocket picked in Bangkok soon after we arrived, I did not want to go through the trauma of that again. After half-an-hour of this we had had enough (though I think Bridget had had too much before we started!), and came back on the underground, but I was glad to have done it.

On the way back to Bangkok, Bridget was upgraded to business class again and this time I had an aisle seat with a neighbour who thought that both arm-rests were for him! However, after two hours it was all over, and Bridget had to go through more interrogation with the immigration authorities before they would let us go on our way. You would have thought that they would have been pleased to see her back! Glad to be home after four days away of non-stop sight seeing, we were very tired and although it was 2 a.m. we stayed up talking to Ed for some time.

We were both impressed with Hong Kong. The infrastructure works, and works well, the streets are clean, public transport is efficient and reliable and the road signs are clear making it easy to get around. The people are friendly and helpful and though luxury items are expensive, everyday items on the whole are not.

A memorable few days.

CHAPTER 19

Phuket, February 2005

For the three-day half term this month, we decided to visit Phuket, the Thai island which was devastated by the tsunami of 26 December 2004. There were few visitors, and many hotels were offering some good deals, as well as reduced air fares to attract at least a few tourists. Were we taking advantage of other people's misfortune? Or should we go in order to help fill the void in their cash flow? We went to a decent hotel which was high on the hill overlooking Karon beach, and we paid 150 pounds for three nights, including return flights.

From the TV and news reports I imagined that all of Phuket looked like Aceh in Sumatra, with all dwellings demolished and boats flung far inland. But this is not so, and of course there is serious damage to the sea-front hotels, restaurants and shops on the west coast of the island, which gets worse as you go further north, and then on to the mainland at Phang Nga, which was flattened. We were on the south of the island, and our resort was made up of chalets, none of which were below 100 feet above sea level, and so were untouched by the waves. For anyone who had booked a holiday here from abroad, it is quite understandable that they would want to cancel, as the reports on TV showed cars, boats, tables, chairs, trees and bodies all lying about in great rotting heaps. Not many people would be altruistic enough not to cancel, though there were charitable souls who came out and helped clear up the mess, and their work was greatly appreciated.

So the beaches were empty of foreign tourists, though they are slowly filtering back now. Where there should have been five or six rows of sun loungers on the beach there were only a handful out, and only a few of those were occupied. In Patong, the Benidorm of Phuket, I was reliably informed that at this time of the year the sand is almost invisible under the rows and rows of chairs!

The beaches are beautiful, long and white, the sand is clean and the water is warm and clear. Having had a lingering and rather expensive lunch with suitable beverages at a restaurant that had escaped the worst of the damage, we enjoyed sitting on the beach and swimming in the sea. I scored a first by observing some topless sunbathers – almost unheard of in Thailand. Mind you, it has to be said that those who were doing it definitely should not have been! The sand here has a peculiar quality to it because walking on it sounded just like walking on freshly packed snow – a slightly squeaky sound. We found out the reason later: there are JCB diggers on the beaches at night under arc lamps digging 10 to 20 foot holes, and then backfilling them. They are working their way across the beach looking for bodies – there are still thousands unaccounted for among the 300,000 missing. So the sand, having been dug up, has not been compressed by many feet above the normal tide line. Apparently, people come out to watch as an after-dinner activity – how sick is that.

All aspects of tourism are down, which was shown in one of the most enchanting trips that I have done. We joined a party on a boat for 24 people, on which there were only four others, which we reached down a long and rickety pier to a small ferry that got us to the boat. We steamed peacefully across a clear sea, with a slight breeze cooling the hot sun, to arrive one hour later at some limestone karst islands off the north east coast off Phuket island. We anchored and transferred – none too delicately in my case – to a rubber canoe, two passengers and an oarsman, which went into the caves of the islands. During spring tides, we would have had to lie flat in the canoe in order to gain entry, but not that day as it was a neap tide. The spring and neap tides vary as much as four metres, and when the tides are at their highest, some caves are completely under the sea. Once in the caves it is totally black, and although the boatman had a torch it was a mystery how he found his way. The ceiling was covered by somnolent bats which we could see, but not hear, and there were thousands of them jostling for space to hang. We were advised to keep our mouths shut if we looked up!

We came out into a lagoon with the limestone walls stretching up 200 metres or more in nearly sheer cliffs. Trees and shrubs manage to cling on to these walls somehow, and the effect is like something out of Jurassic Park. Over a couple of hundred million years or so, rain had washed away at the top of the island, while the sea encroached from the bottom eventually finding its way inside, thus forming a lagoon. It is unbelievably quiet in there, and the peace is only broken by birds twittering to their own echo and the gentle slap of the paddles on the water, and there is absolutely no wind. Monkeys sometimes make their presence felt with their noisy chattering, but not that day. Sea eagles and kites live here too, and glide gracefully in the updraft over the lagoon, while mud flappers acted out their ancient role as one of the links between sea and land creatures. Most of the islands are worn away at sea level so that from certain angles they appeared to be floating, and stalactites dripped from the overhang like icing melting off a birthday cake.

As we sat in the restaurant of the hotel, well above sea level, and looking down on to the length of Karon beach below, we wondered what went through the minds of guests having breakfast at 8.30 on the morning of Boxing Day 2004. There they were, planning their day's activities and outings, when below an increasingly large wave swept over all the chairs that had been laid out on the beach and on into the shops, restaurants and hotels on the front. Before the waves came the sea receded a most unusual distance, exposing the sea bed that no one had ever seen before, and many people went out to see what was going on, and I expect I would have gone too, to look at the exposed coral beds. This is what happened to one of Bridget's colleagues from school. She was walking with her husband, son and his girlfriend, and three of them perished, leaving only the traumatised girlfriend who had clung to a tree, and spent several days in hospital with severe lacerations, which were not only to her body. An extraordinary story to emerge was that of a teen-age schoolgirl who had been learning about tsunamis in her geography lessons the week before. She recognised that the unusual behaviour of the sea indicated that a tsunami wave travelling at something like 400 miles per hour was imminent, and shouted to all those nearby to run for high ground. It is not known how many lives she saved, but it must have been quite a few.

Thailand's endemic problem of corruption is not seen by tourists, but newspaper reports of aid going astray are common. One overzealous officer in charge of handouts said quite clearly that she was not going to give any money to anyone she did not recognise – so tough if she did not know you. The PM here, who had just secured a further four-year term of office with an increased majority, has refused to accept offers of aid from other countries because 'Thailand can look after itself, thankyou very much.' So the government is funding those made destitute from its own coffers, and the distribution seems to be quite arbitrary. The enormous sums collected by voluntary contributions are not being refused, and one can only hope that these will be speedily and fairly administered.

A natural disaster of this magnitude is an awesome thing, and can cause such misery. These things have been so remote from me before, and coming here has brought it much closer, and I fear for those people who live on or near the earth's fault lines. Something is bound to happen sooner or later. We are so glad we went to Phukct, and we saw parts of what the 'Pearl of the Anderman' should be like, and we saw what happens when nature intervenes.

One of the reasons that Thais are not going to Phuket and the area is their fear of ghosts. They are sure that if a dead body is not dealt with in the proper manner very quickly, the owner hangs around until his body is buried, and only then does he become free to pursue his next life. So the perception is that there are thousands of ghosts lurking around Phuket waiting to move on. When Bridget told her class that we were going there, many of the children and their parents were quite shocked and surprised, but I don't see how this will ever be resolved as there is no way all the bodies will ever be found.

CHAPTER 20

Hanoi, Vietnam, April 2005

With the realization that we were shortly to leave South East Asia, and had not yet visited Vietnam, we took four days of the Easter holiday to go there. We bought guide books and talked to people who had been, and settled on Hanoi in the North, and in particular the Old Quarter of that city. We more or less stuck a pin in the guide book, and booked a hotel online, so with flight tickets and plenty of US dollars, we set off early on Monday morning. We were met at the airport, and transported to the Lucky Star hotel and then up 75 steps (no lift) to a comfortable en suite room on the top floor, and had a very small balcony from which we were able to view the busy street below and the interesting roofscape opposite.

Our first impression of Hanoi driving was horrific! Horns constantly blowing, near suicidal overtaking and confrontation at crossroads and intersections seemed to be the recipe for mass carnage – but we saw no fatalities, no crashes and not even any scratches and bumps! There are masses of motorbikes, all of which have their own agenda on the roads, in fact rather like Bangkok. Crossing the road on foot certainly appeared to be a perilous undertaking, but we soon realized that nobody actually wants to run you down, and if you pursue a definite course, all vehicles will go round you. Being irresolute is the best way of getting knocked over.

We took our first tentative steps in the streets in search of a beer and went in to a café selling Bia Hoi which we had been advised to try. As it was on the first floor, we had to climb some very rickety stairs with the distinct smell of rats in our noses. There were sure to have been cockroaches lurking about as well. Nevertheless, we took a seat on the balcony and watched the lively street scenes below while enjoying the beer – which was rather sweet for my taste, but at about 30 pence for a half pint, I managed to force it down! While there we had a bowl of very glutinous soup which we hoped was not a foolish move, but we suffered no ill effects.

While there the weather was overcast, with a little drizzle at times which was fine for sightseeing and walking around because it was not too hot – in fact I wore a light anorak which I have not needed for 7 years in Bangkok. We did lots of walking in the Old Quarter of the city where we found that many of the streets were named after the trade or profession which is being carried on there. We found shoe shops, hairdressers, jewellers and silk shops, to name but a few, all clustered together, and we were grateful that the 'Tin Smith' street was not near the hotel as the constant tap-tapping was irritatingly persistent!

The architecture of this part of town is very French, because of course Vietnam was a French colony for nearly 100 years until 1954, and many of the houses, while not exactly crumbling, are in need of maintenance. Narrow and tall is the general style, being only one room wide – even detached or semi-detached houses. We visited the Memorial House, a renovated dwelling which shows how merchants and other middle class people lived 50 or more years ago. The front room from the street led through to a living area and the kitchens. Upstairs was the dining room (plenty of servants to carry the food upstairs) and a prayer room, and beyond that there were bedrooms leading out from an internal open-air balcony. The lavatory downstairs was a 'squat' loo and a concrete tank nearby was filled with rainwater and was used for bathing, though if this was the only source of water it was not quite clear what the arrangements were in the dry season. All this walking necessitated many 'pit stops' in order to take on liquids of some sort. We walked into the Café des Arts where we enjoyed a delicious appetizer and a carafe of wine. The French patron was charming and loquacious with a good command of English who found that his style of life in Vietnam with a Vietnamese wife was all he wanted from life. A happy man. When we tried to talk to him on life in a communist country, he wouldn't be drawn and became a little less outgoing, though still very entertaining.

The US dollar is the universally accepted unit of currency, but we needed some Vietnam money for drinks and so on, and the exchange rate is in the order of 15,000 dong to the dollar. Not for the first time did I ponder on why the authorities did not just divide everything by 100 or even 1,000 and introduce a few coins. All the notes are filthy and torn and the smallest and filthiest note I saw was for 1,000 dong – about 4p.

We felt obliged to go to the Water Puppet Show largely because the guide books were full of it, and we had been told by others to go. It is unique to Vietnam and was started by peasants for their own amusement in the paddy fields. I am not a great fan of puppets, but one has to admire the technique of the puppeteers who stand in a large tank of water behind a screen and operate the puppets on the end of long sticks. The hour-long performance was made up of short scenes portraying scenes of Vietnamese cultural life, a lot of which has a strong Chinese influence. This is not really surprising as the Chinese ruled the area for over 1,000 years, give or take the occasional uprising, and have left their mark here as they did everywhere they went. But we watched a very colourful spectacle of dragons dancing on water, marriages and funerals and boats whizzing about without crashing into one another.

A good way of seeing a city in a short period is to buy a guided tour, and this we did. As it was advertised to collect us from the hotel at 8 o'clock, we got up in good time but had to wait for another hour before the mini-bus turned up – 'Mai pen rai' or never mind, as the Thais say. This was our first morning, and we had been looking forward to some lovely fresh French bread or baguettes for breakfast, and we were disappointed to be given ordinary sliced toast with our egg. However, we found out that the waiter would go out into the street and stop a passing bread seller as and when required, and so for the next couple of days we had excellent breakfasts! Great.

Our first visit was to the Ho Chi Minh mausoleum to see 'Uncle Ho' lying in state. We thought there would be a queue for ages, but we were moved quickly through being hustled along by soldiers in ill-fitting uniforms and none too politely either. Why do communist countries have to honour their founders in this way? It seems a bit gruesome, and it is said that Madame Tussauds have a hand in his upkeep - he might as well be a wax-work for all any one knows! He appeared to be a benign and peaceful old man whose mission in life was to oust the French from his beloved country, and when they had gone, to get rid of the ruling classes. Having achieved this, he settled down to a firm but not despotic rule. The whole area around this ugly concrete edifice containing Ho is given over to all aspects of his life, and is set in peaceful park-like surroundings. He worked in a winter house with heating and a summer house which was open to cool breezes, and all his pens and books are set out on his desks as he left them. He led a solitary private life, and he never married and was often to be seen walking in the gardens which are now a public park. The shade of the trees, and the lakes in the garden were in complete contrast to the building which contains his body. In front of the mausoleum is a large parade ground area which is presumably used for patriotic assemblies and the like.

It was interesting to see the faces of the Vietnamese tourists. Many – or most – of them appeared to be from the countryside, with weatherbeaten faces and gnarled hands, on their long awaited trip to see their hero and saviour Ho. There are some 80 million people here in Vietnam, but only about three million of them live in the cities, so the the urban and rural communities are in great imbalance, and farming is by far the largest occupation of the people.

In one of the outbuildings we came across a delightful group of musicians playing ethnic instruments. Two of these in particular took my attention: one was a single-stringed instrument where the length of the string was governed by the little finger of the right hand, while the player plucked away with his thumb and forefinger. A vibrato effect was made by altering the tension of the string, which was attached to a flexible mast, by using the left hand. It was not nearly so complicated as this sounds! The other instrument was a set of bamboo pipes arranged horizontally, which was activated by a light clap from the musician's hands to create a puff of wind. Very clever, and very tuneful.

The teachings of Confucius are very old, very traditional and clothed in mystery. We visited a seat of learning for his teachings, and at the temple at the far end of five courtyards, each dedicated to a different aspect of his teachings, were rooms for study, and several figures of the Master. Each of these courtyards contain rows and rows of steles made of marble, which are gravestone-like slabs engraved with the names and accomplishments of celebrated past students. This place was mainly for the instruction of mandarins who had to pass stiff civil service exams before they were able to practise, and the teachings of Confucius were basic to the knowledge and application of the law, and to the administration of the country.

Earlier, we had been to a Buddhist Pagoda, where we learnt that Vietnamese temples were devoted to people while pagodas were devoted to prayer. Here there was a funeral in progress, and a monk was chanting prayers while a host of mourners sat around on the floor all wearing white cotton bands round their heads. They didn't seem to mind us being there as the guide kept on talking and we stepped over their legs! We continued, after an indifferent lunch, to walk round a market. An enormous

155

covered area, there were all kinds of goods for sale both to traders and the public. Bags, shoes, hats, domestic goods, clothes in all shapes, sizes and styles and bales and bales and bales of cloth, in as many colours and materials as you could possibly imagine, were there for all to see, not to mention leather goods, fancy items and ceramics. A lively and colourful atmosphere with people bustling about hither and thither as is the way of markets.

On an island on the lake in the centre of the city stands the Ngoc Son temple and this is reached by a red painted wooden bridge in Chinese style. The temple is also in the Chinese style, decorated with lots of red and gold paint and fiery dragons, which is all quite startling. It contains many Buddhist artefacts and the preserved remains of a 200-year-old turtle which died a few years ago. Its mate still lives on in the murky depths of the lake, and it is said that should you be lucky enough to see it, you will have everlasting good fortune.

That was the end of our trip, and the next day we visited the Ethnology Museum which was a large building set in open land on which was displayed ancient dwellings and ways of life. Inside, the development of the people was portrayed in an easily understood way in several languages. An interesting footnote to this outing was that the taxi driver had no idea where the place was, and so he kept on having to ask people. He couldn't read my map, and I wasn't sure where we were anyway, but the bonus was that we saw parts of Hanoi that we would not otherwise have seen. Much wider streets than in the Old Quarter are lined with cafes and houses painted in bright colours, but many are in need of maintenance.

On one of our 'pit stops' while walking round the Old Quarter, we met an Englishman who was running the establishment. Over a convivial carafe of wine, he was very chatty and explained that he took in 'street kids' and taught them how to wait at table and serve customers so that they could go on and get jobs in tourist areas with the help of a little basic English as well. Mind you, he was paying them next to nothing, but at a dollar a day it was a fortune to these boys and girls. The education system here, he told us, was in a bad state. There are a couple of International Schools which are mainly attended by ex-pat children, though there are probably some important officials who manage to get their children educated there as well. The demographic pattern is that 70% of the population here is under 30 and there are far too many children for far too few schools. In order to avoid classes of 80 – 100, schools open six days a week with two sessions of five hours each, and either your child goes to school in the mornings or the afternoons. Efficient use of school buildings is what they have, but it is hard on teachers, as there are not too many of them either.

Hoa Lo prison which was built by the French 100 years ago for political prisoners is now a museum. As the revolutionary fervour in the early years of the twentieth century grew, so did the inmates of the prison, though during the Second World War the French had other matters occupying their attention, and the Japanese came in as an occupying force. They returned in 1945 expecting to carry on where they left off in 1939, but the Vietnamese were far more organised now, and finally got rid of their colonial masters in 1954. The history depicted here by the Vietnamese tells that the 'heroic' rebels were treated to all sorts of indignities at best, and horrific treatment, torture and death at worst. Prisoners were regularly beaten, beheaded by guillotine (on show) and shackled by their ankles on concrete beds. It all looked pretty gruesome, and women and babies were also kept there regardless of the needs of the children.

The communist North under Ho Chi Minh, having thus been instrumental in independence then started to wage war on the hopelessly corrupt capitalist regime in the South. This is when the Americans stepped in, in 1964, as the North became so successful in their campaign, in order to try and prevent what they saw as a communist take-over of the whole of South East Asia and beyond. During this time US airmen were imprisoned in Hoa Lo, and were treated much better than the French treated the Vietnamese and very much better than they deserved as an invading force. According to the historical notes in the guide, the brave and heroic revolutionary guards behaved according to the Geneva Convention towards their prisoners of war at all times. Of course. When the war ended in 1972 the Americans all went home in good health of body and mind.

As a footnote to all this, the North carried on their campaign and the South capitulated with the surrender of Saigon (re-named Ho Chi Minh City). Many fled to wherever they could to escape reprisals from the communists, and finished up in Hong Kong, Taiwan and to a lesser extent Australia, and other nearby countries. In the nearby Women's Museum, which is dedicated to the role of women in the world in general and Vietnam in particular, there are tableaux showing how women maintained the tunnels which were the supply routes of the military. In one such tableau there were women constructing a deep pit, with spikes at the bottom, to catch enemy soldiers who tried to investigate too closely what was going on.

Always eager to try the local brews, on the way back to the hotel we stopped at a very French-style café where I ordered a black filter coffee. Now, I like strong coffee, but this was so strong and so finely ground that the hot water was cold before it had finished filtering into the cup – and it was disgusting! A beer would have been better, but the alluring smell of roasting coffee was so strong when we went in, that my choice was made for me. Passing a square soon after this, we stopped to admire the statue of King Ly Tuai who reigned when the Chinese finally left in 938 AD after 1,000 years of occasionally broken rule. Quite surprisingly in a communist country, he is in the top ten of Vietnamese heroes of all time, and he stands with his head held high in this nicely landscaped little square with seats and a place for reflection.

After three nights and four days, we found ourselves in a large and singularly uninteresting building waiting for our plane home. In the few shops there, the attendants seemed more interested in their manicures than their customers, so we left them to it, and had a beer. The pace of life is slower than in Bangkok, and on the face of it the people seemed content and happy, though as a tourist one cannot really tell, and it is certainly not something that you can speak about. We found them most friendly, and we were able to communicate to a very small degree with a little basic French from time to time.

A successful visit, and if we come to Vietnam again, we would like to go to the hills to the north and west of Hanoi, to Ho Chi Minh City in the south – and to see the country in between, including the supply tunnels of the Northern soldiers.

CHAPTER 21

Returning to the UK

At the end of the summer term in July 2005, it was time to come home after seven years in Thailand. Arranging for shippers to come in and pack everything up was not nearly so traumatic as when we did so at Merriams Farm in 1998, and we arranged to spend our last night in the Marriott Hotel where we have had so many enjoyable boozy Sunday lunches.

We said goodbye to many of the good friends that Bridget had made amongst the parents of her pupils, and they threw a lunch party for about 100 in which they all stood up in turn and extolled her virtues in the classroom. Her children all came together and sang her a lovely farewell song, and it ended with the presentation of a gorgeous sapphire and diamond pendant. Bridget had a reply which she found difficult to deliver, but it was very well received by the parents, who all wished us both lots of luck and happiness while trying to keep warm in the UK!

Saying goodbye to all our golfing friends was emotional too, which neither of us was expecting. After our last game of golf, we hosted the food and drink at the Royal Golf and Country Club, and they said some nice things about us while giving us a photo of the two of us sitting in a golf cart at Majestic Creek, mounted in a frame with a lovely inscription. Later on we had another party for our non-golfing friends at the British Club, mainly colleagues from school.

I have really enjoyed my time in Bangkok, and probably the thing which I will miss most, after some lovely people we have met, is the climate. As I have said, playing golf in shorts and a shirt all through the year is absolutely wonderful, and neither of us minded being too hot, which is infinitely better than being too cold. We shall miss living in a comfortable flat with no gardening to spoil our weekends, and with a swimming pool on the premises. With cheap taxis and cheap petrol, we were easily in touch with the centre of the city where there were several good and inexpensive restaurants, and with the many elevated expressways, the countryside and golf courses were easily accessible as well. What we have missed over the years is seeing the family on a more frequent basis than once a year. Our grandchildren have been growing up without our being able to see them regularly, and of course, neither have we seen enough of our children.

We eventually got back to Heathrow on July 17 where we hired a car until we could get round to buying one, and, after staying with Giles and Amanda for the night, we then took up residence in the same holiday home in Staplehurst that we have had for the last three years, where we shall be until we can get our bungalow in Bearsted ready.

Thus came to an end a really interesting and enjoyable phase of my life.